MAKE
LIFE
SIMPLE

Make your life as simple as possible, but not simpler.

Andrew Gibson

MAKE LIFE SIMPLE

Published by:
Woven Word
An Imprint of Fisher King Publishing Ltd
The Studio
Arthington Lane
Pool in Wharfedale
LS21 1JZ
England
www.fisherkingpublishing.co.uk

Dedication

To my wife, Natalie,
and my son, Alexander.

They are the loves of my life,
and long may that continue.

'Everything should be made as simple as possible, but not simpler.'

Albert Einstein

Foreword

'I'm so busy' is a phrase I hear so many people, including myself, utter regularly. But busy doing what? And for what?

We're always rushing around making sure we get things done. We like to have 'to do' lists and aspire to tick off the items. At the end of the day, when we've hopefully completed everything on the list, has our life improved? Well sometimes the answer is yes, but often you can feel like you're on a hamster wheel, running really fast but getting nowhere. Once one item is completed it is quickly replaced by the next thing vying for our attention.

On other days, you can find yourself in a state of paralysis by analysis, where big decisions seem impossible because they appear so complex.

Andrew's book brilliantly explains both of these phenomena and what we can do to overcome these frustrations through a really simple process. Instead of focusing on what needs to be done and doing it, focus on how we really want to feel afterwards.

I particularly love how the book relates to both business life and to personal life. I was reading the manuscript on a beautiful sunny

'Instead of focusing on what needs to be done and doing it, focus on how we really want to feel afterwards.'

Saturday afternoon, with my children playing happily in the garden and the sound of running water in the background. I was revisiting the section of the book about what do you really want more of, the senses and feelings around that and then planning actions so you can get more of them.

Just as I was thinking how I wanted more afternoons like this, the kids started bickering. I got ready to lecture them about how this is the kind of behaviour I didn't want from them. Then, just like that, I remembered what Andrew had written: if I wanted more afternoons like this, I needed to reinforce the positive behavior from 5 minutes previously rather than haranguing them for their one slip up!

There is already plenty of complexity in the world. Often, books that purport to provide solutions merely add to that complexity through intricate methods of navigation that can leave us no better off.

This book delivers on its title, providing clear and straightforward processes that can help you, as they've helped me, to make life as simple as possible, but not simpler.

Tim Cook

National Director - BNI UK & Ireland

Acknowledgments

I am grateful to so many people who have helped to shape the thinking that I share here. In particular, to my many colleagues in the Solution Focused Practice community.

It is rare to be part of a community that is so overwhelmingly giving in its nature. We are still learning, understanding, and finding new applications. I have had support, guidance, training, and help from many people in SFP and it would be impossible for me to name them all here. Some have had a great influence on my thinking, and none more so than the late Dr Luc Isebaert, and my friend, the late Greg Vinnicombe. Both were massively influential on my journey and in the content of this book. My training with Chris Iveson at Brief in London was instrumental and he helped me see one of the fundamentals of SFP and transformed my practice. Thank you, Chris. Also, I remember very useful conversations with John Brooker, Hannelore Volckaert, Dave and Debbie Hogan, Monika Jacobi,

Kirsten Dierolf, Jan Muller, Sussan Öster, Geert Lefevre, Sebastian Verniuwe, Paut Kromkamp, Lisa Willems, Dr Klaus Schenk, Ella de Jong, Owen Charnley, Steve Flatt, Suzi Curtis, Jim Bird-Waddington, Tim Newton, Paul Z Jackson, Guy Shennan, Dr Mark McKergow, Roy Marriott, Petra Muller-Demary, Annette Gray, Nalayini Thambar, Fraser Smillie, Anton Stellamans, Liselotte Baeijeart, Dr A. Biba Rebolj, Wendy van den Bulck, David Shaked, Rayya Ghul, Dr Peter Lehmann, and so many more.

I am grateful to my publisher, Rick Armstrong, and to Sam and Rachel, the team at Woven Word. Rick has been a friend and mentor to me for many years now. With his encouragement, I share here what I hope are useful tools to prompt more useful conversations.

I am grateful to my colleagues in BNI. The members of Apex in Leeds have given me tremendous support and great stories. My friends Gareth James, Maria Hatton, Rick Armstrong, Niri Patel, Neil Giller, Louise Eccles-Cookson, Nick Forgham, Andy Gorman, Tim Cook and Charlie Lawson have offered great input and encouragement. I must also acknowledge Dr Ivan Misner, founder and Chief Visionary Officer of this amazing organisation for his help and support with so much of my personal and professional development. The core values of BNI are an essential part of the methods I share here. Central to BNI is the value of Givers Gain. It should be human nature to help others and to give without expectation of a direct gain. I salute all involved in BNI for making this the principal core value of the organisation.

I am grateful to one particular colleague in BNI. Paul Furlong is an expert storyteller with his company Opus Media. It was his talk at the UK BNI Director Conference in 2019 that opened my eyes to the concept of story context within an audience. I am grateful to him for all the subsequent conversations and support as I have developed my thinking in writing this book. I recommend his excellent podcast, Rule the World, the Art, and Power of Storytelling, at every opportunity.

My friends Kieran and Lyz Igwe transformed my health by 'fixing my back problem'. The opportunity to play with my son, Alex, when he was a toddler was a result of their diligent support and I still train at Kieran's fit20 gym every week now. My back problem is not fixed, but their approach gave me what I wanted, and my back problems have simply gone away.

I am grateful to all the clients whose stories appear in this book, sometimes anonymised. To my friends as well who have patiently listened to me jump on my soapbox at every opportunity to share these views. I am specifically grateful to the friends who reviewed this book and helped me shape it before publication. As with my first book, Anthea Kilminster has been instrumental in shaping this. Thank you for your amazing support. I am also deeply grateful to Ian Bennett, Owen Charnley, Karen Hague, Karen Cruise, Sharon Milner, Brett Riley-Tomlinson, James Lawther, Seema Bye, Ella de Jong, Mike Massen, Gareth Bottomley, Marianne Smith, Andy Bounds, Emma Thomas, Ramu Iyer, Louise Eccles-Cookson, Aniela Tallentire, David Burnard, and Gerry Andrews. Thank you all for your help.

In addition to those who helped with early drafts, I am grateful to the many friends who have shared useful conversations with me. These include Robert Campbell, Jim and Ceri Laird, James and Chris Lawther, Alan and Sophie Matthews, and many more too numerous to list.

I am grateful to my wife's family in Australia for their kindness and for welcoming me so warmly for so many years. To my parents-in-law

Tom King and Stasia King, to Stasia's partner Zed, and my sister-in-law Nudge, brother-in-law Chris, and their children Finlay and Katelynn. I particularly want to thank my wife's uncle, Barry King, for his excellent golf coaching which features later in this book, and his daughter Sonia King for her support and encouragement.

I am eternally grateful to my parents, my sister and her family. Mike and Margaret Gibson brought me up with a focus on helping others. Jenny has put up with me the longest of anyone as her big brother and has a great talent for supplying a healthy dose of common sense. And her husband Paul and my nephews Jordan, Mikey and Adam are a joy to be with and a source of constant support.

And finally, to my beautiful wife and son, Natalie and Alexander. For listening to more of my rants than anyone should need to suffer, and for being partners in conversation over the dinner table. I could not have written this without your encouragement and support. Thank you, with all my love.

Contents

Introduction 1

Make Life Simple 9

Three Questions for a Good Life 30

What Do You Want? 47

Change is Out There 59

The P-Myth 76

What's the Difference? 97

Social Capital 115

Building Social Capital 127

Getting Things Done 156

Conclusions 171

Resources 175

Introduction

Four of my friends met for lunch and the conversation turned to 'who do we think is the happiest?'. One of my friends later told me that they all agreed that it was me, yet on every common measure, they were all better off than me. I earned the least amount of money, drove the oldest car, went camping for my holidays. The reason given was that they had all noticed I was happy in myself. I was happy in my work, happy at home, and happy with life. This got me thinking.

In our daily lives, most of what we want is happening most of the time. We are surrounded by good news stories if we look for them. If we make a conscious effort to look for what we want, we will maintain our health and wellbeing. We can take a life that appears complex and most of the time we can keep it simple.

Within our families we all get along most of the time. Occasionally parents and teachers will need to have words with a child who is ignoring them or to correct their behaviour. If those conversations took 15 minutes in a day, for the 23 hours and 45 minutes of the rest of the day, everything is ok. Is it fair to label a child 'badly behaved' if you spend 15 minutes a day having strong words with them? If we are clear about the behaviours we want and compliment them when we notice them doing them, wouldn't that work better?

At work, the most successful teams notice that most of their operation is working well most of the time, and recognising what is going well is vital to maintain perspective and morale. If every meeting starts with the problems and issues, the mood is set low. If we look for people to blame when things go wrong, we add stress and anxiety to a situation that is already tense. If we look for what we want instead, we can strive for more of that. Problems and issues are reduced by a sense of perspective.

Albert Einstein said:

'Everything should be made as simple as possible, but not simpler'

His idea was that we should keep even the most complex things as simple as possible, without losing their essence, and that some things could only be simplified so far without losing something essential. In our modern world, we have moved away from this principle. As a society, we have embraced complexity and seem to take pride in finding complex solutions to complex problems.

The need to act or be seen to be acting has made life complex and expensive. We take action and then review the outcome, and if we don't get what we want, we take another action. This approach runs our lives from small, daily decisions to major changes. We look to 'do something about it!' first. Big data projects are in progress around the world seeking to mine the information we share on-line every moment of the day. The tech companies have a dream that by analysing all the data available, they will somehow unlock human potential, and use this information to boost everything from productivity to politics. Fortunes are made through the perceived value of this activity. Yet every extra piece of data adds complexity, and while we drown in information, we thirst for knowledge.

What if we could work out the outcomes we wanted first, and only then do something about it? Would that make life simpler?

If we could do that, we would do less and spend less, and yet enjoy more of what we want. We would save time and money and benefit more. The methods I share in this book will help you develop this as an approach. If you apply it consistently, it may even become your thinking style.

When we face a challenge, we often look inwards for the answers. We seek an understanding of our nature. We look for tools that help us with our thoughts and personality and a whole industry has built up in the area of self-improvement. We look to improve ourselves by filling ourselves with knowledge about how we work and hope that will make a difference. I propose a simpler way.

Though it might be attractive for some, we are not isolated on a desert island. We live in a complex network of interactions with others. Instead of looking inwards, seeking change, and expecting this to make a difference, let's look outwards for useful interactions. The resources we need are within our networks, and useful interactions are all around us every day if we look for them and notice them. These interactions make a difference every day. To make a change, look outwards first. Change is out there waiting for you if you notice it.

Our society has created and rewarded complexity. Many people have built careers that benefit from this complexity to earn high incomes. These people are considered successful, yet is this what we want for society?

We value complexity and pay dearly for the brilliance of others when we need their input. If their input takes a long time and is very complex, we pay more for it. Shouldn't the simple solution that gets us what we want more quickly be worth more to us?

We equate happiness with 'success', and success is often measured by our label, or by the amount of money we earn. We are conditioned to pursue the most important sounding and highest-earning career. We all want others to see that we are successful, so we give ourselves a fancy job title, or spend the money we earn on things that give external signals of our success. We think that other people care about the car we drive, the clothes we wear, the holidays we take, and we buy expensive items to meet this need. Whole industries have been built around this psychological need.

Is money the true measure of happiness? If so, how much do we need to be happy?

Often the happiest people are not the highest earners. Instead of worrying about money, and what others think of us, we can notice when we make a difference and be happy that we have done so. Our reputation and our legacy are the difference we make, and if we start noticing when we make a difference, we can draw satisfaction from this. We build a legacy through this process of helping others and making a difference. Simply earning more money is not enough on its own for happiness, hence why the richest people in the world are also many of the greatest philanthropists. It is human nature to want to make a difference, and the difference noticed by others we interact with is how we will be remembered.

We worry too much about how things might be, and about events that are outside of our control. It is interesting to look at long term aims; however, you are only in control of your next step. Change is happening everywhere all the time. Trying to keep up with everyone's change as well as manage your own leads to stress and anxiety.

This book will give you simple tools that you can apply to improve your immediate situation. Make the next step, even if it is only small.

We will explore the subtleties of looking for differences that we want before we take action to get them. We will explore stories as your narrative and their power in your network. We will all thrive in a world where we make a difference for others, and where the difference we make is noticed. You don't need to be a billionaire to make a difference.

When we need to get things done, we will go on a journey that will take us to the future, then the here and now (or the recent past), and then we will take one small step forwards to where we want to be.

We will experience an approach that will make your life as simple as possible, but not simpler.

This book is pocket-sized, highlighting the method of concise simplicity. If you think this book feels thin, that is a good thing. Do you want a complex book that is hard to understand, takes a long time to read, and is hard to put into effect?

What do you want instead?

Make Life Simple

I offer this book as a simple method of making progress that does not involve analysing and understanding the problem. This book will help you make progress towards what you want instead.

My proposal is simple: let's put the desired outcomes before the actions.

Let's ask, 'what do we want?' and explore that first. This sounds simple, but in practice, it isn't easy as the desire to do something is very strong. I propose we slow down and think about the differences we want before we act. This book will give you a structure to help you think first, act with confidence, and get more of what you want more of the time.

When you have mastered this, my best hope is you will save time, save money, and get more of what you want.

The method applies immediately when we have a problem, a goal, or a challenge; when we need something to change. Before we take action, we need to know the noticeable differences we want after we have done something about it. You will be able to consider the outcomes you want first and then take confident steps towards them.

This sounds like a sensible way to live, and I guess you might be thinking you do this already. My observations are different as in all walks of life, I see people putting the action first. We always feel the need to 'do something' about the situation.

To illustrate this, consider the movie, *Raiders of the Lost Ark*.

The movie is set in 1936. The Nazis are seeking the Ark of the Covenant as they think this will make them invincible. They have equated invincibility with global domination so this would help them with their quest.

A professor of archaeology, Henry 'Indiana' Jones Jr. is set the challenge of stopping them.

The film follows a pattern. There is a challenge, action is taken, and the plot develops. After each action there is a review. The situation is usually getting progressively worse for our heroes (Indiana Jones and his team), while the bad guys (the Nazis) seem to be winning. When the team is in trouble, they turn to Indiana.

One of the team will ask him, 'What do we do?'.

Indiana will propose a solution in the form of an action to take.

Having taken this action, the team find themselves in a more perilous situation.

Once again, the question is asked, 'What do we do?'.

Again, Indiana issues an instruction, proposes a 'solution' and action is taken.

As the movie develops, so Indiana is placed under increasing levels of stress. Yet still he is asked, 'What do we do?'.

While Indiana and his team are busy trying to interrupt them, the Nazis are making progress towards their quest.

Often, when the team is in serious trouble (usually involving his fear of snakes), Indiana is not capable of proposing an action. Someone else such as Marion, the very capable woman in the team, is asked instead. She proposes an action, and so progress is made.

Despite Indiana and Marion's best efforts, the Nazis reach the Ark of the Covenant. I hope this doesn't spoil the film if you haven't seen it, but when they open the Ark, they do not get the invincibility they sought. Quite the opposite!

This makes great movies – but is it the way we should live our lives?

Raiders of the Lost Ark is a great work of fiction, so we can look at it as a metaphor.

The original quest was set by the Nazis, the bad guys in the film. Their logic was that they were seeking world power and global domination, so if they were invincible, they would certainly win any conflict. Someone in Nazi Head Office suggested that the Ark of the Covenant would enable them to become invincible. A project was developed to obtain the Ark, and unlimited resources were committed to this goal with the expected outcome being 'Invincibility'.

While Indiana and his team did their best to disrupt them, the fictional Nazi project continued on plan. They found the Ark of the Covenant, but when they opened it up, the outcome was not what they expected.

Unfortunately, they only worked this out at the end of the movie, after spending all the time and money on their quest. Their goal was achieved – they found the Ark – but doing so certainly did not bring them invincibility!

Action movies are great fun for many of us, but do they tell us something about how we live our lives? Have you ever done something to fix a problem and then discovered that the outcome wasn't what you wanted?

For example, do you recognise any of the following?

- The person who changes job to earn more money, but is still unhappy at their new place of work;
- The family who moves to a bigger house, then miss their friends and neighbours;
- The couple who separate or divorce, then get back together a few years' later;

- The expensive purchase made, used once, and then left gathering dust at the back of the cupboard.

If you are seeking help, do your friends advise you about what to do? How do you choose the best suggestion? What do you do if the action taken doesn't work?

We often take a similar, action-oriented approach to help others in need. For example, when a friend has a problem and shares their story with you, have you ever suggested what they should do about it? How do you know it's a good thing for your friend to do? Do you base this on your own experience?

When you go to your line manager with a challenge you face do you ask them what you should do? Do they tell you what to do? Does that always fit with your own idea?

If you are the line manager, do you find yourself having to come up with solutions and instructions? How do you evaluate all the available options and propose a course of action that all present can follow? If you are told what to do by your manager and you think there are better options, how can you respectfully challenge an instruction from your boss without losing your job?

In politics, professional politicians are determined to be 'doing something about' the problem. They challenge their rivals with, 'what are you doing about this?' Journalists will ask the same questions about 'what are you doing about this?', and they will report a 'failure to act' or seek to 'hold people accountable for their actions'. Should our politicians always have to 'do' something to 'fix' things?

In many cultures, changing your actions part way through is seen as 'changing your mind'. It is as if you haven't thought it through properly. You are 'admitting defeat', or you risk 'losing face'. Because of these labels, many people stick with their decisions even though the evidence suggests it would be better to change course.

As John Maynard Keynes famously said, 'When the facts change, I change my mind. What do you do, sir?'. We should be allowed to change our minds and do something else. If we pause before we act and think of the differences we want first, we give ourselves the chance to change our minds about how we get these later.

The problem starts with the desire to 'solve the problem'. It is widely accepted that if you analyse the problem and then take action to solve it, you will get what you want. This applies equally to challenges, goals, and any burning desire for change.

The flaw is that the 'solution' to the 'problem' is equated with the 'action taken'. A typical approach would be, 'What are we going to do to solve the problem?'. Only after we have 'done something' do we review to see that the outcome is 'what we want'. To see how that usually works out, please go back and watch, Raiders of the Lost Ark!

This approach constrains us to what we can do, and our ability to do it. We try to change ourselves, or we tell people what we are going to do about it. When we ask for someone's help with a problem, we seek out and commission someone by asking them 'what we should do', or if we are being asked, we advise them to 'do something'. We specify how we want them to do it like experts in their world. When we don't get what we want, we are told that we got what we asked for!

I suggest we change the order to the one that works. Let's look for what we want first, and consider it separately from taking action to get it.

We will learn techniques to identify what we want, describe it in observable ways, and then look for the useful interactions that will help us get what we want. We will work out the action steps afterwards. When we take them, we will know that they are working quickly. We will be able to change our minds and our actions while keeping sight of the differences we want.

Working this way will help us grow in confidence, notice our resilience, and will help us make a difference for others as well as ourselves.

Over time, our stories will develop in our networks. We will see the benefits of having this as a resource we can invest in and draw on in times of need. We will live a life that is as simple as possible, and not simpler.

Here are the elements we will explore in detail in this book.

1. Three Questions for a Good Life

Dr Luc Isebaert was a highly regarded neuro-psychotherapist and world authority for brief therapy. One of the therapy tools he developed was, 'Three Questions for a Good Life'.

Dr Isebaert's advice to his patients was to ask these three questions once a day for two weeks.

1. What have I done today that I am happy with?
2. What has someone else done that I am grateful for? (And did I react in a way likely to encourage them to do something similar again?)
3. Using all my senses, what do I notice around me that I am grateful for? What can I see, hear, feel, smell, touch, taste that I am grateful for?

The idea of these questions was to help the patient focus on the things they wanted which broke the cycles of negative thinking that had brought them to his consulting room.

This simple tool can be applied in many ways and on many occasions.

If you are feeling stressed or anxious, you can ask these questions of yourself. Do this for two weeks. You should notice an improvement in your mood and a reduction in stress and anxiety.

You can ask these questions of your family. If you take time to sit together for a meal at least once a day, these are great questions to ask everyone. I especially recommend asking these questions of young children. Some time spent in their world will enhance the mood of most disheartened adults!

If you are involved in a team, ask your colleagues these questions when you get together. In meetings, these questions are a great way to raise the mood before discussing the challenges of the day.

It is especially important to ask these questions in times of challenge or hardship. Too often, we are drawn into negative thoughts where we think everything is going wrong. Ask these questions of yourself and others. You will see that most of the time, most of your world is pretty much as you would want it to be.

2. What do you want?

When you feel hungry, do you ask yourself what you don't want for lunch? If you are with friends in a café, do you ask them what they don't want to drink? You would need to ask a lot of questions before you placed your order! For simple day-to-day items like a choice of hot drink, we know precisely what drink we want and how we want it.

And yet in major parts of our lives, many of us have still to work this out. By not knowing what we want, we fall into things that tide us over while we work it out. The longer we spend in situations that we don't want, the greater our risk of stress and anxiety. The greater the negative impact on our long-term health.

We live in a world of rolling news, most of which is presented as bad, and this feeds our stress and our anxiety. For example, the news will report 'unemployment' figures when they are high and will make a big news story, yet they seldom make the same noise when 'employment' is as high as it has ever been.

The recent Covid-19 Coronavirus pandemic was the greatest disruption to our society. This was relentlessly covered by all media and social media channels. To listen to the news was to hear of ever-increasing diagnoses and deaths in countries around the world. None of this was what anyone wanted. Work continues to try and understand the disease and its infection and transmission characteristics so that medical cures can be proscribed. While in the middle of the crisis, politicians and many others are busy trying to tackle the outbreak and be seen to be in control of events. This is an almost impossible task, and I sympathise with all who are trying to keep us safe and healthy. While those in charge are wrestling with the problem, there is a simple word that we all can use when we are immersed in things we don't want:

Instead

If someone you know is presenting with things they don't want, ask them what they want instead. For example, if you don't want to catch Covid-19, that is perfectly reasonable. Focusing on what you don't want, you might take the following steps:

- Lock yourself away and not go out;
- Seek comfort by eating sweets and chocolate, or drinking alcohol;
- Avoid other people so as not to catch Covid-19 from them;
- Listen to the news so you can keep up to date with latest developments.

These will all help you avoid what you don't want. But what happens if we ask what we want instead? A good answer would be 'to remain healthy'. When we think about being healthy, we might take the following steps:

- Be sure to take exercise, and if possible, fresh air;
- Drink lots of water and eat well so we maintain our fitness;
- Give other people space when we see them in case we are infectious;
- Look for the good news stories and focus on all the amazing things others are doing to help people through this crisis.

What you want is within your control, while what you don't want is not in your control. Seeking it creates stress and anxiety as these commonly arise when elements of your life are outside of your control. To live a simple life, let's work out what you want.

3. Change is Out There

When presented with a challenge, we often look inwards to make a change. We decide that to improve we need to look at ourselves, do something, do something different. If we change something about ourselves then all will be right.

This approach is hard and leads to us taking big actions. The natural thought process is that if the problem is serious, we need a serious solution that is hard to implement, but that complexity will make it worth doing. This results in people moving to a new house, changing job, or leaving their partner and their children to fix a problem. Sometimes it works, but it would be great to know we were making a good decision before we acted.

Gregory Bateson was a social anthropologist who worked in the mid-20th century who died in 1980. One of his great contributions was to observe people and their interactions with others. He spent time with different groups of people and simply noticed the useful interactions in their society. He didn't try to create them or change behaviours, and he proposed the following:

> *Change is happening around us all the time. If we notice the change that is useful and amplify it, we will make progress towards realising more of what we want.*

As a Western scientist, Bateson worked in a period where indigenous people were being 'discovered' and 'studied'. Experiments were designed to understand human civilisation, and the traditional scientific method applied. Develop a theory, design an experiment to test the theory, then experiment. Finally, compare the results with the original theory. Experiments involving indigenous people conducted this way would inevitably change the behaviours of those who were being studied.

Bateson took a different approach which was considered radical at the time.

He spent time with local peoples in New Guinea and Bali where he observed their interactions. He noticed those that contributed to society and as much as possible, he consciously minimised the impact of his presence as an outsider.

His central theme was that society depended on useful interactions. People interacted differently with different people and in different circumstances. There were no innate 'behaviours' that lead to people acting the same way in all interactions. From this, he developed a simple principle: 'Notice useful change and amplify it'.

This has developed into the next step in this process. When you know what you want, you can notice times when you get it, even just a little. You can notice what is happening at these times and then do more of it. This works if you look for the helpful and useful interactions that surround you. Useful interactions are reduced by social isolation due to retirement or illness. It is important to recreate new versions of the useful interactions that helped you in the recent past. Creating new connections with people you can interact with is a great way of maintaining your health and wellbeing.

4. Differences Before Actions

We often set ourselves a goal, or we are regularly given them at work. They are nearly always in the form of an 'action'; a desire to do something or to achieve something. Have you ever achieved your goal, and then thought to yourself that this wasn't what you really wanted?

We need to separate 'what we want' from the 'goal'. The goal is not the action we take to reach the outcomes. To do this, we should express what we want in the form of noticeable differences.

I was taught Solution Focused Practice by my late friend Greg Vinnicombe. He taught that a difference was noticeable if it had the following characteristics:

- Specific
- Observable
- Measurable
- Interactional
- Time-related

Here is a simple example. If a friend says they want 'to be happy', how can we help them? Chances are, their happy and our happy will be different. Instead of offering suggestions based on our own experience, we can ask them to tell us theirs. 'If you were happy tomorrow morning, what would you notice?'. Then ask, 'What else?'. We can ask this many times so our friend builds a list. This creates a detailed picture of what they would notice if they were happy. Asking them to think about a time in the future helps them to think about a time when things are different from now. This makes it easier to consider and to describe as it takes our friend out of their current situation. We can help them describe their desired future, and then help them take steps towards it.

One of the answers might be that they would be smiling. We can ask what others would notice too, and perhaps they would notice your friend smiling. Our friend would notice them smiling, and it is possible to see this in the moment it happens. If they wanted to, they could keep track of how many times they noticed people smiling in a given period. 'Being Happy' is a Goal. 'Noticing people smiling in a day' is a SOMIT difference. We separate the two and life becomes a lot easier.

5. Time

Change is happening all the time. Change has happened in the conversation just completed. Change will happen in the period between now and the next conversation. This awareness can help a parent expecting a child to instantly respond to their guidance or correction. Give them a little time to adapt and change so you can notice the change you want.

We need to realise that change happens in between conversations. Change is happening out there, and all the time. Notice the change you want and amplify it. You will need fewer meetings. You will have fewer conversations to 'emphasise the point'. You will have less disciplinary conversations with your children (though I can't promise you won't repeat yourself a few times!).

If you allow for the passage of time in between conversations, you will build capability in those you help. A great sign of this would be to notice that they don't come back with the same questions, challenges or problems.

6. Social Capital

Humans are storytellers. Anthropologists estimate that we developed language skills around 700,000 years ago. The earliest form of writing found is Cuneiform, found on Samarian tablets, and estimated to be 7,000 years' old. For most of our time on Earth, we have been telling stories. Storytellers were instrumental to the survival of every tribe, and stories would be passed from village to village, from generation to generation. Useful stories helped people learn from others, and to build reputations. Stories about you and your reputation in your network is known as Social Capital.

When we are aware of Social Capital, we notice how our narrative develops in our network. We can influence how we are observed through the actions we take. We can notice when we make a difference. More usefully we can notice when others make a difference.

We can create and nurture our story and others' stories. Being a useful person in your network pays dividends that are more than just financial. Building the Social Capital of those around you is a great way of making a difference in your world.

In this book, I will help you develop and apply this for yourself, your loved ones, and your network. I hope this will help you make life simple.

Three Questions for a Good Life

Solution Focused Practice

The principles I include here are from 'Solution Focused Practice' (SFP). There are many books and training courses on SFP if you wish to find out more, so this book is not intended as a training manual. I wish to apply the fundamental principles in ways that are simple to adopt.

In my opinion, Solution Focused Practice differs from other conversational approaches in two very specific ways.

- Looking for noticeable differences we want first;
- Looking for useful interactions with others.

These are extra steps before we take action, and when applied to everyday thinking, they are transformational. The fundamental change is that the solution is the difference you want. It is not the action proposed or taken to get that difference.

Imagine the scene in the Indiana Jones movie. We have a problem. The question normally asked is, 'What are we going to do about this?'. The emphasis is on the 'to do'. Sometimes the action will be instinctive as fight or flight responses kick in. That is normal and our survival has depended on this response for millennia, but we are rarely faced with a temple full of snakes, or a perfectly spherical rock rolling after us!

When we make decisions in daily life, we are programmed to act, to ask about 'the to do', and then to take action. We do this, then we review. Have you ever found yourself regretting the action you have just taken as it didn't get you what you wanted? This is where SFP offers an alternative approach.

Noticeable Differences

When people train animals, the focus is on rewarding the behaviour they want. If you teach your dog to sit, and it sits on command, you give it a treat, say, 'good dog', and pat it. The dog learns that sitting on command will result in reward and so learns to do it next time, and the time after that. We probably think we do this all the time ourselves, yet, we spend a lot of time worrying about what we don't want.

So, if our child is misbehaving, we can take action to 'stop the child misbehaving'. Most people do this by talking to their child in the moment, maybe telling the child, 'not to do that'. If they don't respond appropriately, we will tell them again, perhaps more loudly. If raising the voice does not work, we use next steps sanctions such as removing privileges. This escalation continues until eventually the child's behaviour changes. To change the child's behaviour, we have a row, and now they (or we) have changed behaviour. The atmosphere is usually worse afterwards. Now we need to think of ways to keep them amused having denied them the privileges that would have helped us. This is a simple example whereby starting with 'what we don't want', we end up with a result that is not what we want.

When a child is carrying a full cup, how often do we hear someone say, 'mind you don't spill'? This places the idea of spilling in the mind of the child, increasing the risk of spillage. Better to say, 'you're carrying that nicely – well done!' and hope the child continues to carry successfully to the table.

If we revisit the misbehaving child and ask ourselves, 'what do we want?', let's say we want the child to be calm. What would we notice if the child was calm? When did we last notice these things happening? Or in other words, when was the child calm recently? What contributed to this occasion of the child being calm? Perhaps this was noticed after the child was fed, or went to the toilet, or had a sleep or a rest. Maybe now is the time for a snack, a trip to the toilet, or a rest. Parents carry toys and activities with them to provide a stimulating distraction. The child might not know what they want, but the parent can give them something that will attract their focus, even just a little. If we establish calm again, we can then explore the behaviour we want, increasing the chances the child will respond.

So the first activity to develop is to always look for the noticeable differences we want.

Professional coaches and therapists can help clients and patients work out the differences they want as a first step towards helping them. We can help them paint this picture in conversation, then look to notice these differences happening now or in the recent past. When we find them, even just a little, we can build on them. We can then look to move a little closer to what we want. That produces some simple next steps that will help us get more of what we want.

Interactions

The second resource we look for is useful interactions. We focus between the noses, not between the ears. This is key to making progress and also makes progress simple.

As with 'what we don't want', as a society, we spend a high proportion of time looking inwards. We identify people by characteristics seen to be within them, and this often leads to the application of labels.

We apply labels to people from an early age, and we use them to describe behaviours or identify personalities. For example, children can be described as badly behaved, or they can be good as gold. If a child is introduced to a new situation and labelled as one of these, the chances are the adults in the room will modify their behaviour according to the label, rather than to what they notice in the moment. With the first child, they will watch out for bad behaviour and intervene promptly to admonish. They will be on guard to prevent the behaviour they don't want. With the other child, they will notice good behaviour and praise immediately. The label conditions them to notice the behaviours that fit their preconception. The label changes our interactions and can change the outcomes.

Labels can be interesting, they are a useful mental shortcut, and a well-designed questionnaire can be helpful. The challenge comes when the label is seen by others as if it was a problem behaviour. As a simple example, what do you think of when someone is labelled, 'Accountant'? It's a standard reaction to see accountants as boring. Is that true of all of them? Of course not.

For a more serious example, consider our approach to ex-prisoners or ex-offenders. The stated aim of the justice system is to help people rehabilitate. If someone has committed a crime and served time in prison, they are labelled as an ex-prisoner or ex-offender by society. The label includes the time spent in prison or describes the offence committed and doesn't make allowance for the changes the person has made since their crime was committed, or since leaving prison. Many organisations run checks on an applicant's criminal record before hiring them and ex-offenders and ex-prisoners often struggle to find employment. Their prospects are held back throughout their lives.

We make no allowance for the circumstances which surrounded them when they offended. We don't look at the interactions that may have influenced them at the time. We make no allowance for the progress they might make as a result of rehabilitation support. We don't account for the changes in interactions that have happened as time has passed, and meanwhile, the label damages their prospects due to others' perceptions. If we think criminality is hard-wired, what chance do we offer someone to rehabilitate? If we deny someone work, they are more likely to break the law again to make money so they can live. By labelling them 'criminal', we encourage them to behave this way.

I have seen people use Myers-Briggs and Belbin team roles to manage their teams. Recruitment processes use 'psychometric testing' to assess candidates. Large companies are trying to analyse and harvest data in an attempt to develop the ultimate personal profiles of everyone on their systems. All of these are designed to apply labels to people, and we should be aware that these are not always helpful. Whole industries have been created based on the belief that our characteristics and behaviours are internal to ourselves and can be labelled. The reason this often doesn't work is that the label influences the interactions.

We think that a defined personality type will behave in a certain way in all circumstances. This is simply not true. If a child is labelled 'clumsy', adults will take extra care to help them not drop or break things. If a child is labelled 'polite', they will be credited every time they say please or thank-you.

Some labels are genuinely useful and applicable, though they still change our interactions. Let's look at a label that identifies people who are genuinely individual in the way they think: Autism.

There are many identifiable differences within autism where people do think and act in a certain way. 'autism' covers a vast range of differences and there is no single characteristic that is common to all people with autism. For many years, autism was described as 'autism spectrum disorder' or ASD. Thankfully, this label has been changed and is no longer used in mental health practice. The conversation has moved on to discuss neurodiversity instead, where people with autism are simply seen as different from those without who are known as neurotypical. Considering autism as a disorder made neurotypical people think differently and the label sometimes influenced their behaviour. Changing the label from a 'disorder' to a 'diversity' will help us make positive changes to the way we live and work together.

For example, for some neurodiverse people, there are advantages. Some people with autism have a huge capability to concentrate for long periods. Some can take complex problems and solve them simply. Some can interact comfortably with animals. Some can proof-read lengthy manuscripts or software code with absolute accuracy. Stephen Wiltshire PhD was diagnosed with autism aged three. He has a talent for drawing detailed, accurate representations of cities and he does so after observing them only briefly. He is a successful artist and was awarded an MBE (Member of the Order of the British Empire) in 2006. He has talents considered unique and is in demand all over the world for commissioned work.

When a neurotypical person considers autism, it is hard to understand. It is hard to see how a person with autism could fit in with a 'normal' (another label) work environment. As a result, neurotypical people might look to employ people who do not have autism, and hence the label has changed their behaviour.

Those who are employed in a salaried position see self-employment as very hard, or a means of paying low taxes, or sometimes both! Talk to a neurotypical person about helping neurodiverse people become self-employed and this will be placed in the 'too difficult' pile. There is a simple reason for this. The neurotypical response is to think, 'How can I possibly help someone with autism become self-employed?'. We think we need 'to do something' that will help. We then think of difficult labels ('autism' and 'self-employed') that we don't understand. It is impossible for us 'to do something' so we advise that they should do something else that we understand better. The desire to do something to help that is within our understanding creates a barrier to helping. Once again, the labels have changed our interactions.

This label-focused approach reduces the economic opportunity for neurodiverse people. If you look for successful people in every profession, at the top of the tree you will find people with autism. Albert Einstein himself displayed many of the characteristics associated with autism. Many neurodiverse scientists, economists, entrepreneurs, artists, actors and sportspeople reach the top of their professions. They are the way they are. There is no question of them choosing their neurodiversity as a way to behave.

One of my favourite recent projects was to help people with autism explore self-employment. In this project, I worked with the team at Specialist Autism Services in Bradford, UK. In a 12-month project, we helped 33 people, and of these 28 moved on to a 'next step' that was considered progress. Some found employment and some made other beneficial next steps.

With this project, we looked for the times when our clients did something they loved doing. We asked them what they noticed about themselves when they did this. We then looked for when they did this with someone else who benefited. This allowed us to explore useful interactions that were working for our clients. We helped artists, photographers, product designers, charity fundraisers, digital gamers, and many more. When someone else benefited, perhaps there was a value to this? If we could identify the value, there is a possibility of a transaction. During our project, five people concluded this process. Five people with autism were paid for their product or service and took the first step towards self-employment.

No two people are alike, and every interaction is different. We can spend ages trying to analyse the person to improve their 'behaviour' (and as a society we do!), or we can look for useful interactions and try to build on these. This second approach removes the label as it is redundant.

For example, a child is playing with friends and falls over. The child will often pick themselves up and carry on playing. Their friends will encourage them to do so because they all want the game to continue, but before they do, they might glance over to mum or dad. If mum or dad is watching them, and they exchange a sympathetic glance of concern, the child might start to cry and come over for a reassuring cuddle. In my experience, parents learn to look away so their child carries on playing! One child, one fall. The outcome depends on the available interactions.

Think about the number of times you smiled today. Can you tell me precisely the number? It is hard to catch yourself smiling, and even if I asked you to count them and tell me tomorrow, it would be difficult to keep track.

Now think of the number of times you have seen others smile. If I asked you, it would be easier for you to notice others smiling and keep track of that.

And what happens when someone else smiles at you? You smile back as it is infectious, or you notice that it was your smile in the first place that caused the smiles in others.

Three Questions for a Good Life

As an eminent psychotherapist, Dr Luc Isebaert was one of the early exponents of Brief Therapy. A fundamental principle of this is that the intervention with the patient should be as brief as possible. This is stated as 'no more sessions than are necessary', or to put it another way, as simple as possible but not simpler.

As well as developing and training people, he worked as a psychotherapist with a caseload of patients. He used a very simple set of questions and asked his patients to ask these of themselves every day for two weeks and to keep a journal. These are the questions:

1. What have you done today that you are happy with?
2. What has someone else done that you are grateful for? And did you react in such a way that they might do something similar again?

3. Using all your senses, what do you notice that you are grateful
    for? What do you see, feel, hear, touch, taste, smell that you are
    grateful for?

The third question will be familiar to those who practice mindfulness which often starts with noticing your breathing. Consciously noticing your inwards breath, the air circulating within your body, and then the conscious exhalation of the breath is used in therapies to help people ground themselves in the present.

My friend Nick Forgham is a Black Belt in Karate. In his book, 'Black Belt Thinking', he explains that Zanshin is central to martial arts. It means awareness, or literally, remaining mind. He lists Mokuso as a technique to increase awareness and it is a breathing meditation process. Here is how he describes it:

Get yourself comfortable, somewhere you can relax.

Breathe in through your nose and imagine the air you have breathed is a solid object about the size of your thumb. As you breathe in, the breath goes up your nose, up to your forehead, then down the back of your head. It then goes down the spine and tucks under the bottom of the torso, then comes up into your stomach. It then goes up through your chest and comes out through your mouth.

This whole process takes about ten seconds. Then breathe in and start again.

The out-breath is as important as the in-breath, and the technique works best if you close your eyes. If you find just two minutes to do this, you will be refreshed and relaxed. You will have taken time to notice the simplest reflex action and the difference it makes for you.

Dr Isebaert was very happy that people would take these questions in their own way and adapt them. For example, whenever I meet a client or run a workshop, I ask, 'what has pleased you in the last seven days?'. We explore this first and I always like to start a conversation by noticing what is working well before we start looking for the next steps.

1. I take time to notice something that I am happy with today. I can give myself some credit and take comfort in what is going well in my world;

2. I look at useful interactions with others. I can notice that I have

support from my network, even just a little. I consider my own interaction. I can ensure that I give appreciation for the useful interactions. This in itself is something I can be happy with;

3. I look around me and notice what I am grateful for. I realise that while I am coping with my own challenges, there are resources in my immediate environment. I can draw on these for support.

The three questions capture the description of noticeable differences and the useful interactions.

Dr Isebaert's advice to his patients was to ask these questions every day for two weeks. My advice is that you can do the same, more than once per day if you wish, and for longer than two weeks if that is helpful. You can do this with your partner and your family whenever you are together, or with a friend or colleague. These are great questions to stimulate a useful conversation.

You can do this with your team, especially if you are running a team meeting or a workshop.

You can apply these just when you are by yourself and take comfort from noticing what is working in your world.

We will look at the applications of these in the rest of this book, and I will share some other techniques too. While you are reading this book, use these questions and see if you notice a difference.

Now let's help you find more of what you want.

What Do You Want?

'That is Illogical Captain.'

We live in a world that is back to front. We look in the wrong direction. As Dr Spock regularly stated to Captain Kirk in *Star Trek*, 'That is illogical, Captain.' What is illogical? Spending time worrying about what we don't want.

Imagine you went to your local café and you told the barista all the things you didn't want. How many questions would they have to ask before you got the drink you wanted? In practice, we all have our preferred drink and usually ask for the same one every time. Go to the same café often enough and the team will have it waiting for you before you even speak to them.

So when we are faced with a problem or a challenge, why do we worry about all the things we don't want?

We don't want to be ill, for example, so we can spend all our time worrying about 'not being ill'. Or we can look for what we want instead which is to be well. When we start to look for what we want, we can then look for the things we notice in our lives now and in the recent past that contribute to us staying well.

We can look inwards first. Are we well right now? If so, what do we notice that tells us, and what is helping us to maintain this? If we want to be healthier, when did we notice we were healthier in the recent past, even just a little? We can revisit what was happening then and see if we can replicate it, even just a little.

We can look to see what others are doing so that they can stay well. We can copy these for ourselves, and we can notice what is happening around us that contributes to how we want things to be.

Don't focus on what you don't want

Barry King is a great golfer. He is also my wife's uncle. He has played all his life, and even now in his 80's he still plays when he can. When we played together, he used every club in his bag and a few that weren't.

As I was preparing to take my tee shot, he would helpfully advise me, 'Don't worry about that water', or 'I don't think that bunker is in play here'. By doing so, he was planting the water or the bunker in my mind to make me think about them. He hoped to distract me from focusing on where I wanted to aim.

When a child picks up a glass of milk, what happens if the parent says, 'Mind you don't spill that.'? The likelihood of the child spilling increases. The child immediately thinks about spilling the milk. In thinking about it, the child worries about it and spills it. The parent can then state with confidence, 'I told you not to do that!'

When we focus on the problem, we focus on what we don't want. Is that sensible?

- What do you not want for lunch today?
- Where do you not want to go for your holiday?
- What do you not want to be when you grow up?

These questions are nonsense and we would never ask them. Yet we think them all the time. I don't want to be ill. I don't want to be overweight. I don't want to be in trouble. I don't want to be poor.

By focusing on what we want 'instead' of the problem, we take back control of our thoughts and our actions. We can channel them into very specific activities towards something, rather than trying to avoid something.

Sports psychologists advise their clients to focus on what they want all the time. Jonny Wilkinson CBE is the top points scorer in the history of the England rugby union team. He famously envisioned every kick as he prepared to take it and developed a routine that he followed every time. This enabled him to focus on kicking the ball between the posts, and his record is outstanding. In modern rugby, all successful kickers have their own preparation routine and they follow the successful method deployed by Wilkinson.

If the parent noticing the child carrying the milk thinks about what they want, they might say, 'you are carrying that very nicely. Well done!'. When the child is made aware that they are doing the right thing, the chances of them spilling the milk are reduced as they increase their concentration on what is wanted.

If we look at our health, for example, there is a long list of illnesses, diseases and conditions that none of us would actively want. For example, we don't want to catch Covid-19. Let's look at two approaches.

If we think of everything to avoid so that we don't catch Covid-19, we create a long list and we worry. We develop anxieties about these and our stress levels increase which damages our mental health. We might drink more alcohol to help us cope with the worry and this damages our physical health. We might avoid Covid-19, but we end up in poorer health, which is exactly what we didn't want.

Let's turn this into an 'instead'. What do we want instead? We could say that we want to remain healthy. What do we notice about ourselves when we are healthy? We exercise, eat well, stay hydrated, and wash our hands. We have a simple list now and we can consciously exercise, eat well, stay hydrated and wash our hands. If we follow this simple set of steps that are all within our control, we will stay healthy. If we ask the three questions for a good life each day, we will notice that we have done all we can to stay healthy, and our health will improve.

The second approach will not ensure you don't catch Covid-19, but it will ensure that you maintain your mental and physical health in challenging times.

Stress and anxiety arise when we lose control. We worry about things that we cannot do something about and we create our own stress and anxiety. Worry doesn't help us recover control. If we tune into the news or avidly follow social media posts about the global contagion, we simply add to our stress as we worry unduly about things that are beyond our control. We worry about the number of cases or deaths in our country or other countries. We worry about what might happen at some unspecified time in the future when this is over. Will it ever be over? We worry about that too. But I do know that I am in control of how I exercise, how I eat, drink and wash my hands. By focusing on what is in my control, I massively increase my chances of staying healthy in all aspects of my life.

It's not about the 'why'

If you ask someone why they want something, or why they did something, they will respond with a justification. Often their reply will begin with 'because'. Indeed, some children when asked, 'why did you do that?' will just say, 'because', and consider that to be enough! If someone has given you their 'because', it is hard to ask, 'what else?' Doing so challenges their because. The likely outcome is an argument. The attachment to the 'why' is reinforced. The need to do it or get it becomes greater.

Asking someone why they want something moves the conversation towards action which then makes progress harder. We are heading for an Indiana Jones scene whenever we ask someone 'why?'.

However we still want to establish someone's reasons for wanting something and if we are conscious of this, we can ask a better question. When someone presents you with something they want to do, or that they want you to do, don't ask for the 'why?'; ask for their reasons instead.

Frame the question as, 'what are your (good) reasons for wanting <the change>?'. It is easy to hear the client's answer and then ask, 'what other good reasons do you have?'. We can then ask, 'what else?' as many times as possible. We build a long list of reasons.

We help our client build their desired future as a list of noticeable differences. To do this, we accept the first reason given and then we ask, 'what else?'. We keep asking this until a long list is created.

Often, the first reason given is not the real reason. Asking for the 'why?' gives you little to work with. Often the first answer is the one the client or child thinks you want to hear.

Asking for reasons and then more reasons allows the coach or parent to explore in more detail what they want. We can then help establish which of the reasons is most important to them.

So don't start with 'the why'. Start with 'the good reasons' for wanting something.

Are you obese? We can help you lose weight.

I work in a lot of community centres. I often see charity posters offering to help people. They will say something like:

Are you obese?
Did you know that obesity is a cause of cancer, heart
disease, stroke, and diabetes?

We can help you lose weight and avoid these.
Come to our class on Thursday evening
so we can help you.

Each of these is about 'what you don't want'. The reason the poster is written this way is commonly caused by the source of the funding for the project. The charity wants to help people live longer so they have sourced some funding to tackle the causes of people dying. We have funders who are interested in the issues mentioned above, and so the poster matches the stated intention and meets the needs of the funder.

Written this way, the poster is scaring me into engaging. If you think the poster is right to do this, consider my perspective if I was the target audience. I must first admit that I am overweight, then I need to come to a class on Thursday and admit this to a group of strangers too. If I don't do this, I am likely to get one of these terrible conditions. This does often work, and some will engage for this, yet most will put it off until they have a brush with the conditions mentioned. I might be obese now, but I feel fine, so I will skip the class and keep going as I am.

We know that the charity and their funders want to tackle these conditions and help people lose weight, but what about the people they want to engage with? What do they want?

Consider what differences our clients would notice at a point in time after they have successfully lost weight. How about a poster that focuses on what people want?

> *Would you like to play with your kids more?*
> *Would you like to take long walks in the park?*
> *We can help.*
> *Come to our class on Thursday evening*
> *and we will help you.*

We can look for the noticeable differences after our clients have lost weight, and we can look for the interactions with others that would be helpful. It is more likely that people will engage, and they might even tell their friend who also wants to play with their kids more and see if they want to come with them.

It is likely more people will attend on Thursday evening, and once there, you can help them tackle their obesity. Most of them will fit your criteria, and for those that don't, chances are the charity will have other programmes or referral partners that will be able to help.

I recently helped a local school with this approach. They had run workshops designed to help parents cope with stress and anxiety. They were marketed to parents and carers as:

Help your child cope with Stress and Anxiety.

Attendance was low each time. The school had tried running them at different times of day, and in different ways, hoping to attract more families. The highest attendance before my intervention was two parents. I asked what differences parents would notice if their child was not stressed and anxious. We came up with a short list and the next workshop was promoted as:

Would you like your child to be confident and happy?
Would you like them to sleep well?
Would you like them to be able to talk to you about what's on their mind?
Would you like to know what to say when they do?

The workshop was the same as delivered before, but on this occasion, it was attended by ten families.

People engage for the differences they want. Only after they have engaged will they then take action to do something about our situation.

Change is Out There

Throughout our lives, we live and work in collaboration with others. We live in family units, and we often work in teams. Teams that work well together are a joy to be part of, while teams that struggle are a source of tension and stress. We can help our teams by looking for the outcomes we want first, and by resisting the call to act first, or to 'change behaviour'.

There is a challenge to overcome which is we feel that we are under pressure to act or to be seen by others to be acting. We worry about what others think about us. This is a known phenomenon and it is called, 'The Spotlight Effect'.

The Spotlight Effect

Remember the last time you caused someone offence at a party? Or the time when you upset a stranger accidentally? When you forgot to phone your client that day? These are things that cause us to worry.

What will they think of us?

The next time you see the person you offended you might remember the offence you caused. You feel compelled to apologise, yet the other person can't remember what you are talking about.

If a friend can't remember you causing them offence, strangers will be the same. If you did something embarrassing when in a shop or a café, it is unlikely the staff will remember next time you visit. If you phone the client at the earliest opportunity, they will usually be ok with it, and as your project progresses, the missed call will be forgotten.

Yet we worry about these things long after they are gone, and it is the Spotlight Effect that causes us to stick with a decision to do something, even when we realise that it is not the best thing we could do. We worry about what others will think of us if we 'change or mind'. We worry about 'losing face' if our initial course of action is seen by others as somehow being wrong.

The metaphor is to imagine that we all live in our spotlight. We imagine ourselves on a stage with everyone looking at us. We imagine that everyone is in our spotlight with us. Yet the truth is that we are all in our own spotlight, in our own imaginary theatre, imagining everyone looking at us. But if we are all in our own spotlight, then no-one is actually in anyone else's!

The reason our friend cannot remember us offending them is simply that they have been getting on with their lives. In the time that has passed since we last saw them, lots have happened. The best approach when you see them next is to pick up from where you both are now, not where you were last time you met.

Change is happening all the time, all around us, and for all of us. If we notice the useful change and amplify it, life is improved for all and becomes much simpler.

Interaction in the Family

We live in interaction with others, with the world around us, and with the circumstances that apply at that moment in time. For example, if a child displays anger, the parent can respond by trying to exert their authority. We have all seen this from time to time, and if we are parents, perhaps we have done this ourselves. We might respond to our child's anger by becoming angrier. If we ask, 'what do we want instead?', that creates options.

Young children absorb language easily and naturally as they often repeat the phrases used by their parents. As a parent, have you ever caught yourself saying something your Mother said to you when you were young?

We are not born with these words and phrases within us, we learn them from interaction with others.

Interaction All Around

We interact with friends and neighbours, shop assistants, local businesses, and many more. If we are employed we will have colleagues, and if we run a business we will have employees. We may deal with customers and clients, internal or external. Similarly, we will have internal or external suppliers.

We interact with the outside world through many forms of communication now.

If we attend school or college, we interact with our fellow students, teachers and non-teaching staff. We interact with parents and families of other students. We interact with those who help us in other ways to further our education.

In our non-working time, we interact with others even if we choose to take time to ourselves at home. By listening to the radio or a podcast, watching TV, or reading, we will interact with the presenters or characters. They will change the way we behave and the things we say at any given time. This flexibility of approach helps us to change depending on circumstance and it helps others to see us differently depending on the occasion and their own interactional perspective.

Teams work in constant interaction. If we are aware of these taking place within the team, we can make simpler progress. If we are aware of useful interactions with our network of contacts, we can make simpler progress. We can notice and meet our needs and theirs. We can reduce the complexities that arise when we label people and then try to change their behaviours.

Example – Excluded Children

A method of maintaining discipline in a school classroom is to exclude disruptive children. Exclusions can be for a lesson, a day, or for a longer time. In cases of repetitive behaviour, permanent exclusion from school is used as the ultimate sanction.

Karen Cruise works with children who are at risk of exclusion. She coaches them and helps them to make progress so that they can continue their education. In the process, she will often sit in on a class so she can observe. In most cases, the children she is asked to support display an interesting conundrum.

She will notice that the child she is supporting is most disruptive in one class. Perhaps they disrupt when they sit next to a particular pupil, or in the presence of one particular teacher. The child goes to other lessons and is less disruptive. The exclusion system looks at the problem where it is at its worst. As a result of their most disruptive behaviour in specific circumstances, the child is excluded from one class, and sometimes all classes.

If the child can exhibit the desired behaviour in other classes, what do we notice there? What useful interactions are contributing to what we want? If the child can display what we want outside of school, what do we notice there that is useful?

Is it the right course of action to sanction them when one lesson is going wrong? If we look at the possible interactions, we can perhaps take a different course of action.

What do you want?

I have discussed this issue with schools. The process has been to track the occasions when a child is disruptive and to record the occasions when they are excluded. Detailed records are accrued of the classes and lessons involved, and a picture is created where the number of exclusions is recorded per child. There is often a sliding scale of increasing sanction, yet the permanent exclusion of the child from the school is the worst possible result for all involved.

If we ask, 'what do you want?' to the school administrators, they want the child to stop disrupting others. Yet that is actually something they don't want. Asking what they want instead would yield an answer such as, 'for the child to pay attention in class'. Is that happening already, even just a little?

By looking inwards and focusing on what we don't want, the school records and investigates the occasions when they are being disruptive. This will result in the child receiving labels which will influence the behaviour of other teachers in other classes. This will increase the instances of disruptive behaviour as people will look for it. Exclusion from school will stay with them for life. Labels applied at school will impact their self-perceptions and their emotional intelligence, as well as their qualifications and career prospects.

If we identify what we want instead, it is easy for us to look outwards and notice if it is happening now. If not now, has it happened in the recent past? Does it happen outside of school? When we investigate the occasions the child is meeting the required standard in the class, it is easier to help them progress in their lessons. More teachers will look for what is working and praise and encourage. We will get more of what we all want.

This approach gives us areas to explore:

- We can ask the teachers who see signs of progress to advise us what is working;

- We can see which other students attend the classes. Where do they display good behaviour? We can explore their interactions;

- We can look at environmental interactions. When are they displaying signs of alertness, good nutrition and hydration?

- We can make enquiries at home to find out what is happening when the child behaves well there.

Each of these approaches will give us signs of what we want. If we recorded these, we would see the bigger picture. These instances of the behaviour we want will perhaps help us and we can look for the circumstances that deliver better interactions. We can then bring these to the classes which are being disrupted. By looking for what we want, and noticing it when it happens, we will get more of it.

In addition to helping the children, there is a financial benefit to this approach for the school and their funders. It costs more money to support children who are excluded. It disrupts the family which can lead to loss of income which requires more resources from support services. The costs of excluding a child to society include the lifelong impact on their earning potential. By focusing on the problem, we get more of what we don't want.

Working in Teams

When a child needs extra care, many agencies are involved. Multi-disciplinary teams plan appropriate care for the child deemed at risk. The team has representatives of the family, school, police, social work, other therapists, health workers, care workers, advocacy workers, charities, and other interested professionals. Each of these team members will have a different idea of 'what should be done'. If the conversation only discusses action steps, it is hard to reach an agreement. When resources are scarce, it is hard to take away an action from the meeting. It is easier to suggest what others should do. If the team looks at the times when the child is at risk, a long list of risks can be identified. Tackling the occasions when the child is at risk adds complexity, adds risk, and adds expense.

If we determine the outcomes we want first, we make things simpler.

The team can look at how life would be different for the child if they were safe. We can find the occasions when these are already happening. On many occasions, these may be happening when the child is at home with their families already. What do we notice about these instances? Can we replicate the circumstances we want, and transfer them to other environments?

We already have a common example of this in action. A child may behave themselves well at home while with a fidget spinner to keep their hands occupied. If this works at home, could the school allow dispensation for the child to use a fidget spinner in the class? This is a simple action to try, and many schools already do this. We will notice whether the disruptive behaviour reduces.

A great example of this approach is already in use with the 'Signs of Safety' approach. This was developed by Andrew Turnell and his colleagues and is now being adopted by local authorities around the world when supporting children with complex needs.

For many years, we have focused on managing risk and an industry has grown offering 'Risk Management'. There are many techniques to help people identify risks, prioritise them, and then develop contingency plans. A plan is needed for the high impact and high probability risks.

I have sat through or run this process many times as a workshop. The process is to generate every possible risk that the team can imagine. Using a scale of high, medium or low, each risk is then considered for probability and impact. Any risk that is high probability and high impact needs a contingency plan. Similar plans can be developed for risks that are high on one measure and medium on the other.

On occasion, by way of motivation, the workshop facilitator would start by warning us that this was going to be a long and boring process! The generation of possible risks only stopped when someone mentioned 'alien invasion' or 'meteor strike'. As we are noticing in the middle of the Covid-19 pandemic, very few people identified 'global pandemic' as a high probability risk and took steps to mitigate against it. For those that did, the complexity of the problem will have led to a complex contingency plan. If you look inwards and analyse the problem in detail, you develop a well-analysed problem, leading to a complex (and therefore expensive) action plan to fix it.

Identifying every possible, individual risk takes time. Developing plans for those you consider highly probable and highly impactful takes time and resource. What do we want instead? This is the fundamental shift in mindset. What do we want? For children to be safe. Hence, 'Signs of Safety'. The simple question is, 'What do we notice that tells us that this child is safe?'

Andrew and his team developed the Signs of Safety approach when looking after children in 'at risk' situations. The model he developed is now widely used and it starts with the simple premise. When is the child safe? Support services can work with the family to find the occasions when the child is safe and can seek to notice more of these. The family can work towards something that they want, rather than try to mitigate against a long list of things that they don't. It is easier for the support services to look outwards, and to notice and report the factors that are working in keeping the child safe (the signs of safety).

It is easier to manage the care of the children you look after when you look for what you want.

Helping Ourselves and Others

The simple advice to someone stressed or anxious is to talk to someone else or to reach out and ask for help. It's OK to not be OK, and help starts with a conversation or an interaction with another person. If that person can ask you some useful questions about what you want, and what is working, you will start to improve your situation. Dr Isebaert's three questions are a great place to start if you need to help someone.

When people are surveyed about their greatest fears, they sometimes report that 'fear of public speaking' is number 1. Now, I would not recommend asking people about their greatest fears! That creates an inwards looking, problem-focused conversation. But let's work through this as an example. When people ask me for help with a presentation, it is nearly always about their content, their delivery, their fear of getting it wrong. Typically, they will ask me for help with:

- Their script and their slides;
- What to do if they make a mistake?
- What happens if the technology breaks?

These worries are internal to ourselves. We worry about what people will think if we make a mistake. This is very strong when public speaking as it is one of the few occasions when you are actually in someone else's spotlight! Yet even though we are in the spotlight when public speaking, the signs of success are all out there within our audience, not within ourselves, and what we say or how we say it.

If we imagine ourselves attending a talk given by another, what do we notice that tells us it was a good talk? When I ask this question of clients who are worried about a forthcoming presentation, they will usually say:

- People ask questions at the end;
- People take notes;
- People use their phones to photograph slides;
- People will want to speak with the presenter afterwards.

When you are aware of these in advance, you can notice them in the moment. When I speak in public, I notice mobile phones appearing. If more appear as I progress, I know I am engaging with my audience. That gives me confidence that I am delivering for my audience.

If I make a 'mistake' in my presentation, no-one will remember. I can take confidence that the audience wants me to do well. They will forgive and forget far more quickly than I will. Andy Bounds, the award-winning sales and presentation skills trainer, talks about 'the Afters'. He asks his clients to consider what their audience will notice 'after' the presentation or the project. He applies this with all his work, and it is a very successful approach to follow. What difference do you want your audience to notice after you have finished your presentation?

Having looked at the changes happening and at what my clients and colleagues wanted now, I started training people around the world about using Zoom video conferencing. I am helping people like me who train others, facilitate workshops, and manage team meetings to do so using Zoom. One of my workshops did not go well. Within the first five minutes, I lost internet connection to my house, and dropped out of the meeting, leaving my eight delegates without a trainer! When I reconnected a few minutes later, my delegates were happily connecting and talking, and it took a few minutes before they paused to welcome me back! In the same workshop, I was later interrupted by my son, my dog barking at a delivery to the house, and then finally by the gardener using a petrol hedge trimmer! Did any of this make a difference to the outcomes of the course? No. Remarkably, those that attended that particular workshop have recommended me to more people than the workshops where everything ran smoothly. Perhaps that is because they have a more memorable story to tell.

If we look for useful interactions, in every situation, this will help us to focus on what is working. In most aspects of our lives, our stress and anxiety will reduce and disappear if we do this. Turn our focus outwards, find what works, and do more of it.

The P-Myth

The Problem with 'Solving the Problem'

Towards the end of 2018, the football club, Manchester United sacked their manager, Jose Mourinho. Manchester United had made their worst start to an English Premier League campaign since 1990-91. The intention in sacking Mr Mourinho was to improve results and as is very common in professional soccer, it was felt that a new manager would improve the performance of the team for the rest of the season.

According to contemporary press reports, Mr Mourinho was compensated with the sum of £18M to exit his contract. Manchester United then appointed their former player, Ole Gunner-Solskjaer to act as Caretaker Manager for the rest of the season. After an initial period of success, Mr Gunner-Solskjaer was appointed to the post on a three-year contract. Shortly after this appointment, the team's results became inconsistent once more. The overall performance in his period of tenure to date is similar to that produced under the management of

Mr Mourinho. For £18M, no long-term change in results.

This is an example of the most complicated, most expensive, most risky and most time-consuming action being taken to tackle the problem of an underperforming football team.

There have been many studies on the impact on a team's performance following the dismissal of their manager. Most studies concur that for many teams, there is a short-term benefit. This research reports improvement for the six games after the manager has been dismissed. Then, for most teams, performance returns to the level experienced before the dismissal and the team will carry on at a similar level of performance. The problem must lie elsewhere, and so the problem-solving process continues, though often the same action is taken and the manager is replaced once again.

The Problem-Solving Process is The Problem

There is a vast industry built around 'problem-solving'. If someone identifies a problem, they can search for someone to fix it. A consultant will offer their expertise, perform a diagnosis, and then prescribe a cure. The idea is that the client takes the cure and the problem goes away.

In many applications, this works well, and the approach is therefore taken as the accepted method of making things better. When someone breaks their leg and goes to their local hospital, the medical team will swiftly identify the problem and prescribe a cure. When a car is making a strange noise, the mechanic will diagnose the broken component and fix it. On these and many other occasions, problem-solving will give us what we want.

This works where what we want is easily identified as somehow opposite to what we already have. If my leg is broken, I want it to be mended. If my car is making a strange noise, I want it to stop making the strange noise. Where the process starts to unravel is when the problem is complex, or where the opposite is not obvious. If I am a professional athlete with a broken leg, I want to be able to return to the top of my sport. If I think about what I want, I can identify other beneficial activities that will help me rehabilitate more quickly while my leg repairs.

National Speed Awareness Courses

The United Kingdom has a strong track record in road safety. Improvements in vehicle safety coupled with investment in safety infrastructure on UK roads have helped maintain a steady reduction in road deaths since the end of World War II, levelling at around 1,800 deaths per annum since 2012.

In the UK, if you drive faster than the speed limit and are caught, you have two options. The first is to take three demerit points on your licence and pay a small fine. The second is to attend a 'National Speed Awareness Course' (NSAC) and learn skills which will improve your driving. These were introduced nationally in 2008. Attendees are those who have committed minor speeding offences, and the intention is to improve driving standards overall. According to a UK government report, NSAC participants are estimated to be 9 percent less likely to re-offend up to three years after receipt of a course offer.

The course fee is equivalent to the fine and by taking the course, you avoid the demerit points. I was recorded by a speed camera going a little over the limit and I attended a course.

I have always been obsessed with cars and driving. From an early age, I wanted to drive. I read Advanced Driving manuals and the Police Driving Manual when I was seven years' old. I passed my driving test the first time, and I have a passion for driving well. And I enjoyed the training course. The presenters made it fun and engaging, and I learned some useful things that will help me become a better driver.

On the second day, we were asked to analyse in detail the occasions when we broke the speed limit. We were to think of all the factors and to write them all down. The idea was that this would then allow us to correct our behaviour in future. I spoke with the trainers afterwards and they told me that this approach had been designed with psychological input. The theory is that if speeding drivers focused on the times they sped, they would then be able to do the opposite in future and adhere to the speed limits.

As a society, we want people to drive within the speed limit as this is known to reduce road deaths and injuries. My suggestion is that we stop focusing on the times when drivers speed and start focusing on what we want instead.

If we want people to observe the speed limit, a better question would have been, 'Look at the times when you drive within the speed limit. What do you notice?'. We could look at the instances when we leave the house on time or are not delayed by rush hour traffic. We could helpfully look at the interactions. 'Who else is involved? What do they notice?' If the children get out of bed on time and we leave the house earlier, we do not feel the pressure of getting to school on time and so we don't need to speed. By looking for the instances we get what we want, it is easy to repeat them and get more of what we want. Looking at what we do not want and expecting to find the opposite just leads to confusion.

There will be occasions when the children are dropped off on time, and the parent arrives at work early. What happens on these instances? Working through those occasions will give the family the chance to repeat these in future and get to their destinations on time. The need to break the speed limit will no longer arise.

I enjoyed the NSAC, and it reminded me of a lot of things I thought I knew but had forgotten. A subtle change in focus for the final session might make a difference to the outcomes. If the drivers explore what is happening when obeying the law, perhaps they will be helped to observe the speed limit more of the time, which is what society wants.

Complexity Driven Pricing Models

There is a problem with 'solving the problem'. How do you know that you have identified the problem that needs to be solved? If the problem is what you don't want, what do you want instead? Analysing the problem leads to a well-described problem but does not necessarily lead to a solution emerging. Curing the problem after it has been analysed and understood may lead to other problems. There is no end to the process and no guarantee of improvement.

The good news is that the Problem-Solving industry has the answer to this. They have spent thousands of hours analysing and labelling every problem they can think of, and then designing a cure for it. The more complex the problem, the more complex the actions needed to solve it, and the more expensive too.

There is a very good reason for the dominance of the problem-solving approach. If you present with a problem, your friendly problem-solving expert will gladly help you. They will tell you that they have the skills and abilities to help you solve your problem. For them to make income from this, they need to demonstrate their expertise. They will make a diagnosis and recommend a cure and you will pay them to take all the steps necessary for this process.

If you work in an organisation, you will recognise these elements whenever you engage an external consultant with a brief to solve a problem:

- An audit
- Questionnaires
- Interviews with key stakeholders
- External benchmarking
- Market analysis and research
- Process reviews
- Production of a draft report
- Feedback gathering on the draft report
- Production of a final report

This all takes time and resources, all of which costs money, to get to the point where recommendations are made within the final report.

The report will be comprehensive and the value is visible in the large document that describes the problem in detail. You will have paid for all this activity as a prelude to getting the 'solution' from the expert. In my opinion, most of this is a waste of time and money.

Look for what you actually want!

For 16 years I had a problem with my back. And for 16 years, medical professionals tried to 'tackle the problem' by working on the damaged area. One consultant recommended I buy his product to 'activate the lumbar region'. I used the product for many years when travelling or at my desk. None of these interventions 'fixed my back'.

When I first consulted personal trainer Kieran Igwe about my back problem, he asked me 'What do you want?'. This prompted the discussion about the change I wanted to notice in my life. I wanted to pick up and play with my two-year-old son. I wanted to be able to kick a ball and run with him. If you have never experienced a back injury, you may be wondering how it would stop me from doing these things. When you kick a ball, you raise the arm opposite the kicking foot and pull down as you kick. Energy passes through your core to enable the leg muscles to kick the ball. If you have a weak core, this is hard and if you have a structural problem in your back, it can be impossible.

The subtle difference between 'What do you want?' and the more normal 'What do you want to do?' is just dropping the 'to do', yet this makes a monumental difference to the question.

Had Kieran asked me what I wanted to do I would have told him I wanted to 'fix my back':

- Problem = injured back
- Solution = fix the back
- Expected outcome = back fixed

It is natural to focus on the problem (an injured back) then deliver a course of action to tackle that problem. The logical expectation is that the back will be fixed. Unfortunately, focusing on the problem area does not work as 16 years of medical treatment of my lumbar area ably demonstrated.

Kieran reframed the problem by asking what I wanted:

- Problem = injured back
- What I want = play with Alex
- Solution = strengthen the core muscle groups
- Expected outcome = play with Alex

The difference I wanted afterwards was the important thing here. By exploring this first, Kieran and his wife Lyz developed a programme that helped. My injury is a ruptured disc in my lumbar region. The disc has little blood flow in the region and so will not 'fix'. Strengthening all the core muscles supports this weak point, reducing the contribution to core strength it is expected to make when I am active.

The interactional element of my wanting to play with my son provided strong motivation. Strong enough for me to stick with the fitness programme for 2 years. I still work with Kieran now on a maintenance regime at his fit20 gym here in Leeds. I still have an injured back, but I play with and kick footballs with Alex now. The impact of my back injury has gone away, even though my back has not itself been fixed.

Conventional Problem Solving

Here is how we typically make progress. We are presented with a challenge or a problem, an issue and we ask, 'What are we going to do?'. We act and do something about it. After we have acted, we review. Did we get what we wanted?

It looks like this:

Issue → Take Action → Review

I can then review – is my Issue resolved?

a. Yes – Success

b. No – I now have a new Issue – I repeat the process to tackle the new Issue.

We repeat this process many times in a day. It helps us to make simple decisions and complex ones.

I am hungry. → *Eat some food.* → *I am full.*

The opposite of the problem gives me what I want so for this simple example, the process works. Yet this process is used for major decisions too.

I am bored and frustrated with my life.

Shall we move to a new house? Shall I change job? Should we get together/break up? Shall we have a baby?

Many people have moved to a new house, changed job, started or ended a relationship, or even started a family, and then reviewed afterwards. This often works but many people have regretted it and wished they had done something else. By this time, it is often too late to reverse your actions. The opposite of the problem might not give me 'what I want'.

Remove the 'to do'

What if we change the question slightly? We are presented with a challenge. We ask, 'What do we want?'. We consider this in terms of the differences we would notice if we had it.

Here is the process:

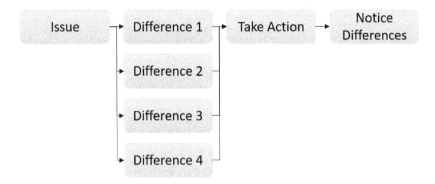

1. I have an Issue.

2. Imagine I overcame my Issue, what Differences would I notice afterwards? What else?

3. Imagine I overcame my Issue, what Differences would Others notice that would tell them? What else? Who else would notice? What would they notice? What else?

We can generate a list of noticeable differences from different perspectives. We can then reference our action to previous experience.

4. Have I noticed these already, now or in the recent past, even just a little?

Then we can imagine we were a small step closer to where we want to be.

5. If I was a step closer to the Differences I want, what would I notice?

It is a simple outcome of this process to identify the simple actions needed to make progress. When you then take action, you can look for the noticeable differences you identified before you acted. Noticing them means you are on track. Not noticing them means you can change what you are doing.

The Merger Opportunity

A friend of a friend was contemplating merging his business with a rival's. Tentative discussions had been held, and he was interested in pursuing the merger. He had held exploratory talks with his accountant and other professionals about the technical aspects of merging. He had started thinking about the deal structure that would be needed and how the merger would be funded. If asked, 'What do you want to do?', his answer would be, 'To merge my company with my rival's.'

In my first meeting, he presented me with this conundrum. It was something he was seriously considering and lots of people were happy to help him pursue this project. He was asking them to help him merge his company with his rival's and they were accepting this and offering their professional help. There was little or no sense check that this action would give him what he wanted. Why would they do that? Their income depended on the deal going ahead, and they were simply doing what he asked them to. The more complicated the process, the more time and resources needed, the greater the resulting fees.

As you will have noticed by now, I don't follow that model.

I asked him what difference it would make to him if he merged with the other business and we spoke about this for an hour or so. We looked at the other people involved and considered the interactional elements. We explored what he and the others involved actually wanted.

As it happens, he and his wife were seeking to reduce their involvement in running their business. His rival and the rival's business partner wanted this as well. The merger proposal relied on existing team members stepping up to run the newly merged operation. The first step was to find out what the team members wanted.

Having identified this first step, we can use this approach to speak to the team member and find out what they want. We don't need to share any plans or suggest we are considering merging the company. We can look for the differences our team members would notice if the business was running brilliantly. We will build their desired future and we can see if it fits with ours. We can then, in private, consider whether merging two businesses is the best action to deliver these.

Thinking it through in conversation this way saves time and money.

Simplicity Driven Pricing Models

In the above example, my conversation was less than two hours in length, yet the difference made was immense. Consider the costs involved in merging two businesses, only to then find out that you didn't get what you wanted. Yet if I valued that conversation on my input, two hours of an hourly rate would be a small payment for such a large difference.

For this reason, people develop complex programmes that take time and resource, and as a result command higher prices.

Consider this scenario. Imagine I could work with your business and generate £100,000 in extra profits every year. How much would you pay me for my help? Would £10,000 be reasonable? If you could afford it, you would probably say yes. 10% of the year one benefit is a fair investment to get the return.

- Option 1. I propose a six-month programme of works starting with an audit and finishing with a final report. The price of this is £10,000. Deal done, let's make a start!
- Option 2. One conversation that lasts two hours. Would you pay me £10,000? Probably not. Yet if I can credibly demonstrate that I can deliver the difference for you, you should.

In this example, perhaps you should pay me more.

If we imagine the £100,000 was to come all at once. You will start getting these immediately with option 2, while with option 1 you have to wait six months. Option 1 is worth £50,000 more to you. If we apply the 10% rule, you should be happy to pay me £15,000 for my help. So why doesn't everything work this way?

The missing factor is credibility. With credibility, some people successfully work with a model that is based on Option 2. For example, if you want a meeting with Warren Buffett to discuss investment strategies, he will rightly charge you a high fee for his direct help. If you have high credibility based on making a difference already for others, this route is possible to follow.

People are attracted to Option 1 because they see the value in the six-month programme. They see the days this will take the consultant and the intellectual property they are buying. As the consultant explains their programme and the thought that has gone into it, the client is convinced of the need for it. They realise that this all needs to be paid for. The discussion about fees is all about what is going to be done to get the difference, rather than the difference the programme will make and when it will make it. The consultant earns a fee, and the client realises the benefit after the end of a lot of hard work. The credibility comes from the programme as explained before the work is done.

From the supplier's perspective, this forces consultants to create programmes that are somehow different from their rivals. It is hard to compare one programme with another, yet that is the process many go through when invited to tender for a project. How do we know which programme will deliver the best outcomes?

My challenge is to help us all realise that Option 2 is usually better. We should be exploring the differences we want to notice first and describing them in detail. Make your interaction as simple as possible, not simpler, and if it delivers the differences with credibility, this should be the better option. If the outcomes are high value, clients should be happy to pay according to the differences made, not the amount of work done to get them. If less work is needed to get better results more quickly, this is worth more money, not less.

To illustrate this, imagine a trip to your dentist. You have a problem and they offer two courses of action. The first will involve two hours' of painful treatment and will cost £200. The second will be less painful and will be finished in 20 minutes. What price would you expect to pay for the second option? If you could afford it, you would pay much more for option 2 than for option 1!

Where the problem is complex and interactional, it is a myth that tackling by doing something will give you the solution. When you try to solve a problem, the opposite of the problem is not always the solution. The 'problem' is 'what you don't want'. Forget about solving the problem for a moment. Remember to ask yourself, 'What do I want instead?'

What's the Difference?

How to Coach an Ice Hockey Team

Paul Z Jackson is an expert coach, trainer and facilitator. He is an author, and a master of improvisation having worked as a producer for BBC Comedy for many years. He was working overseas and was invited to see a local ice hockey match. On hearing he was a great coach, the team asked him to help them. How could they play better?

Paul is a keen football fan but knows nothing about ice hockey. Before the match, he simply asked the team the following question. 'If you were playing brilliantly, what would I notice?'. The team told him some things such as shouting to each other, tracking back, supporting attacks. Paul said, 'OK. I will watch out for these.'. They came to see him at the first break and asked him how they were doing. He said he had noticed them doing the things they said they would. What would he notice in the next third?

The team played their best match and were narrowly beaten by a stronger, older team. They thanked Paul afterwards for his amazing help with the gift of an ice hockey stick. Paul's input was very simple but made a massive difference to the team.

Giving and Receiving Instructions

We ask for help and we expect to be told what to do. We want people to do something, so we tell them what we want them to do and how to do it. We receive instructions from relatives, partners, our colleagues or our clients. When we commission works, we tell the other person what we want them to do. It is amazing what some clients expect me to achieve in half a day's training course!

Let's look at a common aspect of collaborative working – when you are told what to do by someone else.

Instructing another is a complex arrangement. Few people like being told what to do.

The real challenge is when we are asked to do something and we would rather do something else. As a baby, we will refuse to eat the food offered if we don't like it. Before we can even speak, we can screw up our face or turn away. We learn quickly that batting away the spoon works well!

If we work in an action-oriented way, our response to instruction is reinforced as we grow. Children don't like being told to do their homework. Teenagers don't like being told to tidy their room, or to leave their phone alone. We all want to do our own thing as we grow up. To be an individual. Then we enter the world of work.

Following instruction is essential to making progress at work or in business so I do not advise challenging the instructions you receive in the manner of a baby, child or teenager!

Here is a way that I hope helps everyone make simpler progress.

If you are asked to do something, a short check of the differences they want will help you deliver what they want. These questions increase the chances of us getting it right first time. This extra step in the initial conversation saves time and resources.

What Difference Does This Make?

Look at the question above. Imagine asking this of your manager as a teenager would ask it of their parent. This question can be taken as a challenge to authority! For this to work, your manager needs to be thinking the same way as you do. They need to be familiar with this method too.

A good approach is to ensure that we tell our manager that we are happy to accept their task (as long as the task is ethical, legal and fits our values of course!) Accepting the instruction ensures that you can explore further to help you do it well. You can now ask, 'what difference will this make?' to clarify what is wanted. Your manager will help you to see their reasons for asking you. So how do we know we are talking about Differences and not Actions?

Differences have the following characteristics:

- Specific
- Observable
- Measurable
- Interactional
- Time Related

SOMIT for short. In business, we are very used to the concept of SMART objectives. How do they compare? SMART stands for:

- Specific
- Measurable
- Achievable
- Realistic or Relevant
- Time-related

There are many variations on SMART and people have added additional letters. The basic difference is very simple. SMART goals and objectives drive us to Actions. SOMIT goals and objectives describe Differences.

To make things as simple as possible but not simpler, we need to start with SOMIT. This is the key that unlocks this approach.

You will have noticed that the S, M and T are common to both approaches. The key differences are in the Observable and Interactional elements.

When we ask questions about 'what will we notice?' we can refer to all our senses. To be truly Observable, we should be able to sense the difference we want as it happens.

For example, let's apply this extra step before implementing a sales activity to grow our business. We can easily identify that a successful marketing campaign will drive more enquiries. SMART approaches would tell us we need to measure these. This would encourage us to look for hard evidence in the form of data, perhaps supported by system-generated reports. If we follow the SOMIT model first, we will find a long list of things we will notice as the activity is happening. We will notice the phones ringing more, or more email enquiries from our website as they happen. We will notice more interaction on Social Media. These are noticeable in the moment and tell us our activity is working.

When we look at SMART objectives, the original definition of the A was Assignable. Who do we assign to do this? The R has stood for various things about the Results expected with the available Resources. The challenge when setting SMART objectives was to predict the future and then make action plans to deliver it. What can we do with what we have available? This encourages an internal focus when looking for resources.

SOMIT calls for us to find useful Interactions. We are setting ourselves a task and we have identified observable differences we would notice that would tell us it was working. So who else is involved? What would they notice? We can work this out more easily in a conversation ourselves and if we want confirmation we can ask them. We can add more richness to the change we want and build a fuller picture of what we are working towards. We build a list that will tell us we are on the right track. We can make a start, and if we don't observe these signs, we can change our activity easily.

We don't need to predict what result we will realise with available resources at the end of the project.

What else?

If we explore the differences first, we can identify all those we want to notice. We can look for the differences the multiple stakeholders will notice when we have taken action successfully. We can review these in a conversation before we act. Conversations are cheaper and take less time. They allow the exploration of all the SOMIT differences we want before we spend our money.

Take Brexit for example. One reason given for leaving the EU was that opportunities for employment are reduced by freedom of movement. For a parent worried that their child cannot find work locally, ending freedom of movement would logically help. If leaving the EU ends freedom of movement, then my child will have more chance of finding work. This does make perfect sense and is a good reason for voting to leave the EU. This is an example of taking action to get what you do not want. (Note that on this occasion, what you do not want is the desired action and is therefore seen as a good thing.)

So what do we want instead? We want our child to find employment.

Is ending freedom of movement going to help? Well, it might.

Brexit is the most complex, most risky, and most expensive option. If a parent is asked 'So what do you want **to do**?', it is perfectly reasonable to vote for the action that you credibly believe will help.

Now, if the question that was asked was simply, 'So what do you want?', the answer could have been 'For my child to find a job'. It is highly likely that a tailored support package for the child in question would help. We could find out what job they wanted and help them with their skills. We could look for the people they wanted to work with and introduce them. We could help them with employability skills, and if we identified the SOMIT differences that would tell us what was working, we could help them find a job. These actions are simpler to implement more quickly, more easily, and with a greater likelihood of success. Ending freedom of movement may make a difference, but we might also need to assist in an individual case by case basis. Only then will leaving the EU make the difference that the parent wanted for their child.

SMART Goals Change Behaviours

Between 2007 and 2011 I was a BizFizz Coach in Bradford, UK. As part of a broad programme of support, I was one of many people helping residents to start and grow new businesses. There were many support services available and Bradford Metropolitan District Council was testing different support methods to see which was the most effective. Each project was given targets to hit, except for BizFizz. At the request of the BizFizz programme designers, targets were never shared with the Coaches.

The reason for this was that sharing the targets would change the coach's behaviour. The BizFizz approach was to trust the coaches, support them with local management, and ensure they delivered the model properly. Managing the inputs would increase the chance the targets would be met at the end of the period. The other projects using different models were conventionally given their targets.

If you give someone a goal that is action-focused, it will change their behaviour. For example, if I had been given a target of helping 12 new business start in the first year of the project, I would naturally want to 'help' 12 businesses to make their first trade. I might split my target and look for one per month and I would help the clients in a way that made it more likely that they started their business. I would select the clients that I thought had the most chance of starting that month and support them more intensely. I would do this with best intentions, but part of this would be so I hit my target.

According to various reports, the survival rate of new businesses after 12 months is between 10 and 20%. Most new businesses fail in their first year in the UK. Partly as a result of not having explicit targets, BizFizz Coaches were able to focus entirely on what the client wanted and the 12-month new business survival rate for BizFizz projects across the UK was over 90%.

The high survival rate is explained simply. BizFizz coaches were relaxed when a client decided that their best course of action was not to start a business as that was a successful outcome. As a result, only those who decided that starting their business was what they really wanted would proceed. The clients who were likely to fail were helped to do something else instead.

On review after two years, the BizFizz Projects were assessed as the most impactful. More BizFizz coaches were appointed and this became the preferred support method in the city.

Goal is not the same as Difference Wanted

Instead of going straight to the goal required, let's work out what we want. Let's look for the differences that will be noticed when we get what we want. If you take a goal you have for yourself and insert it into the following question:

'Imagine we were 12 months from now and we had successfully...
< achieved Goal > ..., what would we notice?'

You can now build the picture of noticeable differences and start the process with a clear vision.

When working with a team, especially in business, the goal does not need to change. Say we need to hit a certain target for our organisation. As the team leader, we can share the reasons why we need to hit this target and the difference this will make to the organisation. The next step is to then ask the team to imagine that we have hit the target and ask them what differences they would notice afterwards. We can help build the picture of the desired future in ways we will all notice.

Having explored the team members' specific noticeable differences, who else is involved? It is worth taking time to consider other stakeholders, especially clients and suppliers. What about colleagues? What difference would it make for our families? What would they notice if we hit our sales target?

We have taken time to build the collective picture of the company, team, individual and wider stakeholder differences. It is now time to ask for ideas about how we are going to move closer to the target.

We look at the here and now. Have we noticed any of these differences happening? If so, can we replicate the situation and do more of it? That will help us recognise that we have already made progress towards what we want.

Have we noticed any of these differences happening in the recent past? Or elsewhere? If so, can we replicate the situation then, or copy someone else? This gives us more, easy progress to what we want. It is always easier to repeat something that worked than to invent something brand new.

Our final stage is to imagine we were a little closer to what we want. We ask ourselves what we would notice that would tell us. Looking back at our long list of differences, we can identify those that we would notice next. We can create an action plan that delivers these first.

This action plan will be shorter and will deliver the A and the R of a SMART objective. We know that the action is Achievable and

Relevant and also that it is part of our desired future.

The plan that emerges will be a combination of actions that moves us closer to the differences we seek. We can implement these and then review. Start the process again as change has happened since our first meeting.

If this process sounds familiar, it is at the heart of Agile and other project management practices. Agile has applied this to software development for many years. Agile makes small improvements in the software, seeks customer input, and then uses that to determine the next improvement. This constant process of small steps with external input helps and the software industry delivers the systems that are essential to our world with minimal disruption to service.

Try this process with your team, or your family, or your committee. You should find it easier to make progress with fewer arguments, and with less time and resources. Your life should become as simple as possible, but not simpler.

Making Progress in Small Steps

Rory Sutherland is an advertising industry guru and TED talk superstar. He was an early guest of TED and his talks have been seen by millions. I recommend you take 15 minutes to watch his excellent TED talk, 'Sweat the Small Stuff'.

In it, he points out that the more complex the problem, the more complex the proposed solution. He describes a mythical project with a budget of £25M which will never be implemented properly. The implementation is too complex as the implementation itself will create more problems than it solves.

He proposes that people should be given smaller amounts of money to make small improvements. If you give someone £25,000 they will implement an improvement. Give them another £25,000 and repeat this process and you will get to where you want to be much faster and simpler. The trouble is, who wants to be the project manager with the £25,000 budget when prestige and power are associated with the size of your budget?

The UK government is investing in complex engineering solutions to improve transport infrastructure. We are building very high-speed railways and a second rail tunnel across London called Crossrail 2. The proposal to build a third runway at Heathrow has been debated for decades now.

These projects give the impression of doing something on a grand scale, yet there are cheaper proposals that would increase capacity on the rail network. Longer trains and longer platforms could be implemented more cheaply and easily, and improved signalling would increase capacity, but the desire to do and be seen to be doing something grand is all-encompassing. Who wants to be the Politician who boldly claims they are going to build a longer platform to accommodate a longer train, only to be asked, 'Is that all?'

So when we explore this further, the reason given for all these investments is 'to grow the economy'. The expectation is that helping more people make more journeys more easily will boost our ability to do more business.

I have been using Zoom for video meetings since 2017. I meet with people around the world in my Solution Focused Practice community and we are keen adopters of Zoom for international meetings, workshops and conferences. Yet for people who lived near me, if I mentioned Zoom as an option for a meeting, I felt like I was proposing a poor alternative to meeting in person. I had some meetings on Zoom, but most of my meetings involve travel to a mutually convenient venue to work together in person.

And then Covid-19 struck.

With a change in the rules on social engagement, people have turned to video conferencing in droves. Zoom subscribers increased from 10 million in November 2019 to 200 million by April 2020. Having found how easy it is to use, more people are using Zoom, and more are telling me they will continue to use it after the Covid-19 lockdown restrictions are eased.

If the government wants us to have more meetings to grow the economy, more travel does not give us more meetings; video conferencing does. Yet in the UK, we rely on private companies to install internet infrastructure. Broadband and mobile internet infrastructure are cheaper and less disruptive to the environment than motorways, railways and runways and the increase in traffic they facilitate.

But the politicians have told us what they are going to do and have staked their reputations on getting the job done. To cancel High Speed 2 now would be to 'admit' that they had made 'the wrong decision' and they would be pilloried by the media. It would be difficult for them to be seen as changing their minds and to later secure re-election, so the project will continue. As a result of our action-oriented thought processes, the UK will invest £106 billion (latest estimate – final costs unknown) on a project that will probably be obsolete by the time it is finished.

Every time you work out what you want in terms of noticeable differences, you will find ways to get them that will help you change your course of action in response to change that is happening all the time. This should help make your life as simple as possible, but not simpler.

Social Capital

You studied at Eton and Oxford and were a member of the Bullingdon Club. You enjoyed a career in London in PR or Journalism. Before you started work, you were already known to your employers. Your father worked there or a friend of his recommended you. Fellow alumni already worked there, and they had good expectations of their new colleague. These factors make it more likely that you will one day be Prime Minister of the United Kingdom.

On the other hand, you find yourself in changed circumstances unexpectedly. Perhaps you retire earlier than planned or having been an active citizen, you now live on your own and have little or no contact with friends or neighbours. You are not likely to become Prime Minister. Sadly, you are also at greater risk of poor mental and physical health and will likely have a reduced life expectancy.

Sociologists and health economists research this and they are looking at the impact of social isolation on health and economic measures. If we invest in reducing social isolation, will that have a benefit elsewhere? Is it more effective to invest in community-based support than more health workers in hospitals?

This is called Social Capital and we all have it, some more than others. Social Capital is simply your narrative in your network. If your network is sharing great stories about you, you will have high social capital whereas if you have no network, or negative stories circulating, you will have low Social Capital.

People recommend us based on our Social Capital. We find work through word of mouth, whether a new job or a new client. The good word of another is the most powerful tool we have, and high Social Capital suggests you are more likely to be recommended. More people will know about you and think of you when they spot an opportunity to recommend you. When they make their recommendation, they will have a great story to tell which gives their supporting reasons. Social Capital is a very useful resource if you understand how it works and how to use it.

Your Network

Most of us have a network of friends, colleagues, neighbours and so on who know us and would recognise our name in conversation. We can participate in an on-line network by engaging in social media. If we are in business, we will have a network of clients, suppliers, customers and competitors. If we want to make that larger, we can attend networking events, conferences and trade shows. These take place every day in our local area or further afield and make the process of acquiring a large network easy.

Neil Giller spoke about friendships and relationships at the BNI Conference in 2019. He asked the audience how many real friends we all had. When we had answered in the dozens or hundreds, he defined a real friend as, 'someone who is there for you, no matter what, and will help you in your time of need.' This dramatically reduced the number of friends we had initially claimed. Neil's point was that with the opportunity to collect many thousands of 'followers' on social media, how do we know who is a friend? Who is a follower, and who or what lies in between?

To be part of a resourceful network, there needs to be recognition, acquaintance, reciprocity, and mutual respect. The key to unlocking the resource potential of your network is to be contributing to your network all the time. If you contribute to your network, you will find your network is there for you when you need it.

Your Narrative

We live in a society where we tell stories. Friends develop their relationships by sharing stories about each other's friends, and families pass on stories through the generations. Customers tell stories about businesses they have used and these stories directly influence sales. The best type of business comes from a 'word of mouth' recommendation. For this reason, businesses invest in their brand to create stories over time that position themselves in a certain way.

Your narrative is your story as it develops over time. Your narrative 'in your network' is the story told by others about you when you are not there; your reputation, and your social capital.

Every interaction we have with another contributes to our narrative, even just a little. For example, how do you address the Barista when they make your coffee? They might ask your name and write it on the side of the cup. Do you address them by theirs? Do you know the names of the shopkeepers you buy from regularly? Do they know yours?

In earlier chapters, we explored the benefits of considering what others would notice when we had achieved our goal. This consideration applies to the process of building Social Capital. What will others notice about us? Will that contribute or detract? If we could write it ourselves, what would we like our narrative to be?

Take a moment to think about a time when you helped someone recently. Imagine you were telling me that story right now. What would you tell me? In one story, I will learn more about you than you perhaps realise.

I recently met with Ching-te Tsai. He is a Chartered Accountant and has served large businesses in the role of Financial Director. He is charming and engaging, and he describes himself as The Happy Accountant. Ching is a great guy, but what can I talk about with an accountant for an hour? If Ching tried to explain to me his skills and qualifications, I would struggle to remember them. Also, based on these, I would struggle to differentiate between him and any other qualified Chartered Accountant. This applies to all professions and trades I meet. So instead of asking Ching what he does, I ask him to tell me a story. Specifically, I ask him to tell me a story of how he has helped someone recently.

He told me that in the middle of the Covid-19 outbreak, he heard that a colleague was considering shutting their business. They saw no other option. Ching offered a conversation. In two hours of Zoom conversation, he helped his colleague consider their options. They did not close their business. With his help, they found a way of continuing to trade, and this helped them to cope with the crisis. And the final piece of the story is that Ching did not charge for this. He was just happy to help a friend in need.

I know many accountants. If I hear of a colleague contemplating ending their business, I can and will refer them to Ching. When they ask me why they should talk to him, I can tell this story. I don't need to know Ching's qualifications; I need to know he made a difference. This story is about the difference he made, and as it is a good story, it will be shared by his network.

I have asked many hundreds of people to tell me stories over the years. I train others to do this as it is the shortest way to get to know someone professionally. When you answer, the story that comes to mind first reveals core values, passions, and differences made. In one 30-second story, I can learn enough about someone to know whether their core values fit with mine. I can establish their passion for their craft and can refer them to people who need the difference they have already made for someone else.

The best bit about Ching's story was what happened next. He, like me, is happy to help people first and not to worry about where the money will come from. A few days after he helped his colleague rescue their business, he received a call. He had been recommended by his colleagues to another business owner and is now engaged as their accountant.

Had he asked for payment before helping his colleague in a crisis, he would not have been able to help. This story is fresh as a write this. How many people will be referred to Ching in months and years to come by people he just helps?

My accountant, Vicky Newham, runs a very successful practice. She has built a strong business providing accountancy and book-keeping services and she and Ching offer similar services. But Vicky is an expert in helping people recover money from the UK tax office when they invest in Research and Development. I can confidently refer people to her when I find out they have invested in this, and she will help them. She has consistently worked on this area for a long time and has built a reputation for this work.

During the Covid-19 crisis, all accountants were suddenly very busy. Their clients needed help with their businesses, and with accessing the various support schemes created by the UK Government in the crisis. Vicky and her team were out there helping as many people as they could, and often helping people that were not even their clients. They freely gave their advice wherever they could.

I had a catch-up with her recently. She has received more referrals for Research & Development Tax Credit projects in the first month of the Covid-19 project than any previous month. Even though she hasn't been mentioning it herself, her reputation is such that her network has been introducing her for her specialism.

Experts are referred by their network due to their reputation. It usually takes time to become an expert. It takes more time to be a 'reputable' expert. Reputations are gained over time by providing consistent help, by making a difference, and by delivering outcomes. The more people you help, the more word spreads that you are an expert who makes a difference. Over time, you will build a strong reputation. Consider your reputation as a resource. A great reputation is the same as having high social capital.

While building your reputation takes time, it is possible to destroy a reputation in an instant. A well-known example is the story of Gerald Ratner. Having built a large chain of jewellery shops selling value items at low prices, he famously described one of his products as 'total crap' in a speech to the Institute of Directors. Immediately after the speech, the Ratner group dropped in value by £500m. He ended up leaving this company soon after, and he successfully built new businesses and went on to enjoy more success. Nevertheless, his one misguided comment was made in 1991, and he is still most likely to be remembered for it even now, nearly forty years' later.

There are many examples where people pick up a negative story and then sustain it long after the story no longer applies. Product scandals have tarnished brands or products, often with long-lasting effects. People forget the details of what happened, but they remember the essence of the story and that is enough to change their opinion. If people change their opinion of you, this has a corresponding impact on your social capital.

If you are conscientiously building your reputation, you will realise that it has value. Every action you take contributes to it, and it should be taken care of like any precious resource.

Real World Social Capital

'To get something done, ask a busy person' is a well-known saying. Busy people are usually effective at getting things done and being busy is a good indicator that you are helping others. The more they are seen by their network to be getting things done, the more likely they are to be asked to do more. But do busy people go out and tell everyone they are busy? We usually notice busy people by the difference they are making. We hear others tell us stories about them that enhance their reputation. The secret to building your social capital is not to try to enhance your own. Instead, do your utmost to enhance others'.

We have more opportunity to do this than ever before. We have access to our network through technology and social media. We have the facility at our fingertips and if we apply the methods I am sharing, we can contribute to our networks every day.

We can look for what is working when we have face to face conversations. We can consider our direct communications and be mindful of our social media activity; are we telling our story, or telling someone else's? To praise another is a natural thing to do and your network will find it engaging. Try to promote yourself and you will appear boastful. It is hard to promote yourself in a way that enhances your reputation, but if you look for the differences others are making, it is easy to pay them a compliment.

To help us find great stories, we can ask Dr Isebaert's three questions. These apply in most situations where there is an interaction. You can create a post expressing gratitude to another for a difference made. You can compliment others when you notice that they made a difference.

There is no difference between real-world and virtual world social capital. Your reputation is your reputation; however, you do not own it, your network does. It is what people are saying about you when you are not there.

Building Social Capital

Make Someone Else the Hero

Imagine you were telling a story about me, and beginning it with, 'Well, Andrew was telling us about how great he was. There was this time when he was so great…' etc. Does that sound like something you would engage with? The most engaging stories are about someone else. When you tell a story, make someone else the hero. I learned this from Paul Furlong who runs a film making company called Opus Media. Paul's clients include Formula 1 and he has worked with some of the greatest in the film industry. He also runs a podcast called, 'Rule the World: The Art & Power of Storytelling', which I recommend as he and his guests make many powerful points about storytelling.

Telling a story about someone else from the observer perspective makes a story easy to tell, and more likely to be told. Stories that contribute to Social Capital must be shared by your network when you are not there. We normally only share interesting stories about someone else so making someone else the hero is the start of the engagement process.

The Power of Context

Have you ever been scared while watching a movie? When you were at your most afraid, what was happening on screen? Virtually nothing.

We see a hand slowly opening the creaking door. The music builds. The room beyond is dark. We start to imagine what could be there. Tension is created in our minds. We don't know what is behind the door! Our greatest fears come forward. We build our anxiety in the moment. Every scary possibility comes to mind in a couple of seconds. We physically react to our fears. We start curling up, clutching cushions for comfort. We close our eyes – which makes it worse! We reach out to take a grip of our neighbour for comfort and security. The music reaches a crashing cadence, and then…

SOMETHING SCARY HAPPENS!

It is called the 'Jump Scare'. In an instant, we are released from our tension. We might scream or gasp, squeeze the cushion, or make a reflex action to protect ourselves. Even though it is 'just a movie'.

That is Context.

The key to successful story writing is engaging with the audience. Nothing engages an audience more than allowing their minds to fill in the blank spaces you leave to their imaginations. The best, scariest films create space for their audiences to create their own context. My scariest thing is different from yours, yet both can be in the darkened room. When we watch the build-up to the jump scare, we want to know what is going to happen, even though it will scare us.

When reviewing the film afterwards, people might comment that it wasn't that scary. Once the detail is revealed the tension is released. We rationalise and compare with our fears and phobias. Yet the fear we felt was genuine in the moment.

When looking to create stories within our networks, as well as making someone else the hero, we need to tell enough of a story to engage interest. If we go into all the details of how everything in the story was done, we destroy the context. What works is to share stories about the differences people make and the outcomes they enjoyed, and not worry too much in the story about the detail of how they did it.

This applies in life and influences the stories we share.

Ramu Iyer is a job coach in Seattle. He pursued a successful career as a project manager for Microsoft until he decided he wanted to do something else and to make more of a difference. He now works with people with learning difficulties and disabilities to help them find employment.

When I asked him to tell me about what he does to help his clients, he told me it was often hard. His clients need his support and a supportive employer. Ramu approaches local employers seeking work for his clients. The employers often feel they are doing Ramu's client a favour by employing them so they often find minimum wage-paying jobs and it is a constant struggle. When the challenges the employee brings with their condition become too much, it is a simple decision to fire them.

I asked him to tell me about successful clients. He told me of a woman he supports who works for the Seattle Mariners, the Major League Baseball team. She has worked there for 10 years and is a popular and successful member of the hospitality team. The Mariners have promoted her to senior positions. She has featured in stories they have told about the club, enhancing the club's PR. She is making a difference for the club, for the fans and the community. Putting the opportunity this way, if Seattle based employers would like loyal staff who make a difference over time, Ramu can help them find them.

Sharing the desirable differences made by his clients as stories will engage employers. Employers who want reliable, loyal employees will get in touch to find out more. If possible and if there is sufficient benefit, they might find ways of adapting to support Ramu's clients' needs. Of course, there are challenges and costs involved, so this approach is no panacea guaranteeing success every time. However, engaging with the prospective employer for what they want increases the chances of a useful conversation. If the detail of the clients' challenges is shared first, barriers are erected and the conversation and likely outcomes for all concerned are changed.

The Label and Context

One area where context can be found is in the application of labels.

We describe some labels as helpful and others not so much. Read the following list:

- Accountant
- Great Aunt
- Politician
- Surgeon
- Teacher
- Mum
- Layabout
- Big Brother

Each of these labels will have prompted a reaction in you as you read them. And your internal reaction will have been unique to you. This is context in action.

Even my accountant thinks accountants are boring. If we think all Accountants are boring, we might miss out on some great conversations. If we think all Politicians cannot be trusted, we might not vote for the ones that are making a difference in our society.

When we define ourselves by a series of labels that describe what we do, we leave the context in the minds of our reader. When the job applicant described themselves on their CV as 'having the rugged, good looks of a natural-born leader', I imagine they did not expect the people reading the CV to fall down with laughter!

The Context Free Question

When I was a BizFizz Coach in Bradford, we kept to a very pure coaching model. Coaching is different from advising. We were under strict instruction to never advise or instruct our client unless sharing factual information. When a client needed input and advice, we convened a meeting of residents and asked them.

The coach would present the client's challenge anonymously and free of context. For example, we would say, 'A client needs a name for their new dog grooming business. Please can you suggest some names?'. We were trained to remove all description of 'the client'.

I stuck to this model well, except on one occasion. My client was starting a chauffeur drive service targeted at helping exclusively female clients with their travel needs. She wanted contact details for local firms who might be interested. I asked the residents' panel for help.

While answering the question, one of the tables called me over and asked what car she was going to use? Without thinking, I said she was contemplating a Volvo. I left them to it for a few minutes. I gathered the input from six tables, and five of them were full of contacts and helpful suggestions. One table had written, 'don't buy a Volvo'.

Elections and Context

In both the 2016 Brexit referendum, and the 2019 UK general election, the role of 'context' was decisive. Both followed the same approach as Donald Trump's successful 2016 US presidential election campaign. Each campaign successfully used the power of context.

'Make America Great Again' is described by Paul Furlong as the perfect story. It has all the elements needed to engage the audience while leaving them to build their own context.

If you did not think America was all that great in 2016, you could vote for Trump and he would 'Make America Great Again'. What did his voters want? For America to be 'Great Again'. The second part –

how was he going to do it? That does not matter if you believe in him. Trump was competing against Hillary Clinton. Clinton was a lawyer who had served her time in office at the highest level. She had been involved in creating laws throughout her career. She was a former First Lady, won election as a Senator, and had global experience as a former US Secretary of State under President Obama. She was probably over-qualified for the job of US President (if that was ever possible). She fought it the traditional way. She outlined policies, explained them, and answered questions. She said what she was going to do and laid out plans to get these things done.

She was beaten by the four words, 'Make America Great Again'.

The 2016 Brexit referendum followed a similar pattern. The Leave campaign adopted the slogan, 'Take Back Control'. This appealed to voters who felt that they had lost control of elements of their lives. If their children could not find work, or they were worried about EU bureaucracy, the voters could vote to Leave. A successful outcome of leaving the EU would be for the UK to take back control. It was never specified as to what we would be taking back under our control. The answer 'our laws, our borders, our money' was again sufficiently broad as to allow the electorate to choose the ones that applied to their needs. The Leave campaign won the referendum, securing nearly 52% of the vote.

In December 2019, the UK General Election was another example.

The Conservative Party campaigned with the slogan, 'Get Brexit Done'. Their manifesto was published but was deliberately short on detail. Recognising that the UK electorate had voted to leave the EU three years' previously and yet still had not left, their slogan appealed to those who simply wanted to get the Brexit process over with.

The opposition parties took a more traditional approach.

The Labour Party produced a detailed manifesto. It explained investment plans and a comprehensive set of policies they would implement if they were elected. Every day, they launched a new policy document. Every day they went onto media channels to explain and answer questions. This raised more questions than they could answer about how they were going to do all these things.

The Liberal Democrats campaigned on a nuanced policy. If they were elected with a majority (a major stretch from their pre-election position of holding less than 3% of the seats in Parliament), they would cancel Brexit. If they were part of a coalition or partnership government, they would seek a second referendum on UK membership of the EU. This was confusing to voters.

During the election, former Liberal Democrats party leader Sir Vince Cable reminded his colleagues, 'if you are explaining, you are not campaigning'.

Both the Labour Party and the Liberal Democrats suffered their worst defeats in living memory in terms of seats won. The leaders of both parties lost their positions. Indeed Jo Swinson, leader of the Liberal Democrats, lost her seat in the election and ceased to be a Member of Parliament.

The winning parties in each of the examples above knew the power of context to make a good story great. They used an understanding of context to engage with their audiences and achieve electoral success.

People Analytics

A Finnish tractor company was looking to sell their brand-new model to the Soviet Union back in the 1950s. They took tractors to the border and met the Soviet delegation. The Soviets crawled all over the tractor, taking measurements, testing components, and field testing the tractor's abilities. Finally, they came to the Finnish salespeople and said, 'We can see that it works in practice. But does it work in theory?'

A friend of mine told me that Google has a department called 'People Analytics'. Facebook has more data on each of its members than any of us know. Google and Facebook use data to help people target messages and advertising to very specific people profiles. Major consultancy firms offer data-based services to help clients find better candidates for employed positions. They talk about improving management and decision making, finding actionable insights, and even a data-driven approach to managing people at work. Society, and especially corporate organisations values data above all. With the explosion in connected computing and data management, society is heading in a direction where data is all-important. Yet as the above election outcomes demonstrate, it is not the most important factor in success.

It is context that leads to a word of mouth referral, or a recommendation of someone for promotion. It is the story of the difference they made for someone else, or within the organisation already that leads to success. The data might help narrow down your options, but the bigger picture must consider the context.

Differences Made Make a Difference

I am often asked about how to use social media. Most people understand the basics and many are proficient at using the platforms. The challenge is usually finding things to write about, and the intention is often to find more clients or customers and to sell more to them.

When people consider posting to social media, the tendency is to look inwards to find something to write about. We expect to create fresh content and original thought every day, but this is hard to do. This inwards focus results in posts which are about the things the author has done. They are not engaging. They do not get much activity within the network that sees them. Have you ever connected with someone who posts a picture of every meal they enjoy? Often the author runs out of things to say, or people in their network just lose interest.

Some people do have original thoughts. The opportunity to share these on social media is fantastic. Many people publish useful articles with helpful techniques, hints and tips. Full methods are very useful and when shared can help a lot of people.

As explored earlier, there is an easier approach which will help all of us contribute more to our networks. Look outwards.

If we look for it, change is out there. We can notice useful interactions. If you look at your friend's or your customer's perspective, ask yourself what difference you made for them? What did they notice afterwards? What worked? And after a little time has passed, what difference do they notice now?

If you take this approach, it is easier to find stories. If you look around you, you can find places where people have made a difference, and then tell these stories.

A great place to start is with the second of Dr Luc Isebaert's questions:

'What has someone else done that I am grateful for? And did I react in such a way that they might do something similar again?'

The first part of this question gives you the material to create a great story. The second part is what you do with the story when you've created it.

A Story about a Story

I am a member of BNI, the largest networking organisation in the world. In 2016, at the UK Conference, I met Dr Ivan Misner, the Founder and Chief Visionary Officer of BNI Global.

Ivan was a very popular guest of honour, and every delegate wanted to meet him. He made a point of getting around everyone he could, and he was charming in the time he gave everyone. The most popular activity was the selfie photograph. Virtually everyone wanted a selfie with him. He generously smiled for lots of mobile phone cameras.

Ivan was working around the tables before the gala dinner. I waited my turn, and when it came, I thought it would be nice to engage him in conversation. After all, what would I do with a selfie? I was much more interested in Ivan as a person, so I asked him to tell me a story about his travels to BNI conferences. He told me this great story about his recent trip to Vietnam.

He was making his final arrangements with his hosts when he was told he would be allocated security while he was there, for his protection. His instinct was that he had nothing to worry about. He loved the people in Vietnam and the War was a long time ago so he didn't think he needed 'protection'? He politely declined the offer, but his host insisted and the matter was settled.

On Ivan's first morning, he was up early to attend his first event. At the appointed hour, there was a knock on the door. His host was there with his security guard. He was greeted warmly and briefed about the next steps in his journey.

Sure enough, as Ivan emerged from the lift, he found a detail of more security guards waiting for him in the lobby. He was listening patiently to the briefing there when he became aware of noise and commotion outside the hotel. It was 5:30 am. Was some kind of trouble going on?

Ivan's security detail explained that the people outside were here to see Ivan. The reason his hosts had provided security was so that he could be protected – from his fans! He needed a team of people protecting his personal space to get from the hotel door to the waiting car!

Ivan's understanding of the reason for the security was the opposite of the reason it was provided. He was so grateful to his host for anticipating this need. He was able to meet many of the waiting crowd, pose for more selfies, and still get to the BNI meeting on time. He told me a great story, and I have told it many times since.

What makes this a great story?

When Ivan told me this story, he made heroes of his host, the security guards, and those who were organising his trip. He was very self-deprecating in sharing his misunderstandings at the start of his trip. When I tell this story here, I can also make Ivan a hero. He was kind enough to take the time to share this story with me, and I really appreciate it.

Who else do we notice making a difference?

What impression do you have about the BNI members in Vietnam? What positive attributes can you list based on this story? Start listing them and you will come up with a long list of amazing characteristics of people who are only mentioned fleetingly.

We have the opportunity every day to look for and gather great stories. If we engage with people and ask them about good news, or where they have made a difference, great stories will flow. If we share these stories, we are building our network's social capital, and by contributing to our network we are in turn being useful. This will be noticed by our network, will become part of our story there, and then our reputation will be enhanced. We will build our social capital by helping others to build theirs.

Stories about differences made are engaging. The audience will want to know more and will ask how this was done.

Building Your Network

Having started to notice and gather great stories, the next step is to build your network. We can do this in both the real world and online, but 'building' is not the same as just 'adding to'. We need to build a network of strong relationships, not just followers or friends on a social media platform.

First, let us cover how not to build a network. If you reach out to people and immediately sell to them, you will struggle. You might build a vast network of contacts, but if all you do is sell to them, you are simply using them as a marketing database.

If your stories are all about you and what you do or what you sell, you will struggle to engage. Your stories will not be shared, or if they are, the sharing may not be complementary. If all you do is complain, you will make it hard for people to engage with you.

If you want to build your network online, start by building your network's social capital. We can do this by developing relationships, by interacting usefully, and simply by helping people.

There are simple things you can do. If you notice stories of people making a difference, compliment them. You can do this in person, or online. If you notice someone telling a great story on social media, like, comment and share their posts, even if you are not connected to them. They are more likely to accept your request when you send it and might even send you a request to connect too!

In the real world, we can build our network through many activities. We already have a network, and it is not a question of how many connections you have. Your network is a resource if you are contributing to it so start with the network you already have.

In a world dominated by connections and followers, where engagement is measured by likes and shares, it is tempting to build a large network. Before you do, look at the foundations of the network you have built already

Reach out and help the people you already know. You can do this with a simple phone call, and by asking, 'How are you?'. Just touching base with someone is a way of keeping in touch. Ask what's going well. Ask about the things they are grateful for. Share good news stories. Talk about people you notice making a difference. Use the three questions for a good life with your friends, family and connections. It may seem a little strange at first, but the stories will start to emerge.

If you are looking to gather stories, you can also ask for them. Instead of asking about what people are doing when you speak with them, ask them:

'Please tell me a story of how you helped someone recently?'

You might need to put this in some context. With someone you know well in your family, this would be a very strange question to ask! In developing relationships, this is a great question.

The storyteller will talk about a way they made a difference for someone else and it will capture their passions and their core values. This is far more powerful than a prepared 'elevator pitch' which has been repeated so many times that even the teller has lost interest! The story could be helping a child learn something, or helping a neighbour get some shopping. Or it could be a way their business helped a client or a supplier. It could be Ching helping a colleague save their business. It could be Ramu helping people find employment. It could be Andy helping people deliver great 'afters'. It could be Kieran helping me play with my young son. I once asked this question in a group of estate agents. Only one of them told the group a story about helping someone sell a house. The rest told stories of helping others in need, and each story was of making an amazing difference for someone else.

If you are interviewing a candidate for a job role, ask them this question. Their answer will reveal more about them than any amount of psychometric testing or data gathering.

Gathering these stories is easy as we are more natural storytellers than fact sharers. Even if we get the details wrong when telling a story, we will convey the meaning. Our audience will engage and add their context. If you notice your network of useful people and start sharing stories, you will set in motion a chain reaction of positive and productive social capital building. On the other hand, if we try to relay facts and actions, it is very important that we get these right and it is hard to do this consistently and engagingly.

Being a Useful Person in Your Network

So how does sharing stories about others help you? By making someone else the hero, your credibility is enhanced as well. Your network will credit you with taking the time to tell the story. You don't need to mention your involvement. By leaving the context to your audience, they will work it out for themselves and in their way.

There are many ways you can be a useful person in your network through the products, services and customer support you provide. You can increase your usefulness by sharing stories. You can increase your usefulness by noticing the differences others make. You can contribute in a way that is likely to encourage them to do something similar again.

The Spotlight Effect and Social Media

In a previous chapter, we explored how the Spotlight Effect influences our behaviours and activities. In summary, we worry about what others will think of us. The Spotlight Effect reminds us that we are all too worried about what others think of us to be worried about what we think of others.

This is especially useful when looking at social media activity. Removing the physical interaction seems to lower inhibitions and as a result, many people feel it is their place to offer criticism, or even be offensive and insulting. The lack of face to face contact seems to make a difference here. When we are with someone or in a group, most conversations are polite and respectful, and there is seldom a need to worry afterwards about what was said. If someone does offend, an apology will usually be sufficient, or the group will smooth it over and return to their equilibrium. On social media, the situation is very different. The simplest way to consider this is to remember the old phrase, 'less said, soonest mended' and move on.

A friend of mine looks after marketing for his company and as a result, he is responsible for social media activity. He was once drawn into an online argument that he felt crossed a professional boundary. No law had been broken, but he was concerned about this to the point where he reported it to his manager the next day and offered to resign. His manager thanked him for his openness and simply told him not to worry. If the conversation had stopped, it would soon be forgotten. If today's newspaper is tomorrow's chip wrapper, in social media, the memory fades even more rapidly if you let it.

If someone passes a critical comment on your post, don't worry and don't engage. Look at the positive comments that this post or your other posts have garnered. Don't dwell on one critical comment if 99% of them are supportive.

If you engage in an argument on social media, you will never win it. Most social media 'debates' rapidly degenerate into trading insults or an escalating war of words. The desire to 'have the last word' on a topic is strong, however if everyone wants this then the conversation will never end, it will only escalate. Indeed, the author Mike Godwin proposed 'Godwin's Law' in 1990. This states that whoever makes the first comparison to Hitler loses the debate that is in progress, whatever the topic! So try not to engage with these conversations as you will add to your stress and anxiety. If you keep engaging and keep arguing, your social capital could be harmed and your carefully built reputation will take time to grow again.

A Story about a Story – Part 2

Ivan told me the story about his trip to Vietnam in 2016. I have told this story often, including to rooms of people on training courses. One of the people who heard this story from me was Gareth James, the owner of Clockwork Eye Video Productions, an expert in video marketing and a colleague in BNI.

In every BNI chapter weekly meeting, we take time to cover a short topic for our education. Gareth came to my chapter's committee in September 2019 and asked to deliver the education presentation in the last meeting of the year, just before Christmas. The topic he was going to cover was 'Being Specific in Your Referrals'. We were a little nervous. Gareth is a stand-up comedian in his spare time. As the meeting before Christmas is always a relaxed celebration, we were sure it would be fine.

When the appointed meeting came, Gareth set up a video ready to play in the meeting. The opening screen was of Gareth talking to camera with his Clockwork Eye template screen. So far, so normal, but Gareth was euphorically happy before the meeting, and we could all tell he had something up his sleeve. When the Education Topic slot came round, Gareth leapt to his feet and pressed play. He started filming us as the video played.

After a short introduction on the screen from Gareth, he introduced Dr Ivan Misner! Ivan had recorded a video message, especially for the BNI Apex Chapter Meeting. We were blown away. Ivan's tips on being specific with our referral requests were very helpful. At the end of his talk, I was very surprised when Ivan finished by saying a specific hello to me. He described me as a good friend that he had met in Windsor, and personally wished me well.

I was amazed that Ivan had remembered me, one of 270,000 members around the world. So how did this happen?

Well, Gareth had contacted the BNI Global team in the USA and asked if Ivan could deliver an education topic for our chapter. Ivan gets messages like this all the time and is happy to oblige so there is a form to complete with the topic and the occasion. There is space on the form for shoutouts to people in the room.

When Gareth completed the form, he decided it would be nice if Ivan gave a shoutout to me. The reason? Gareth knew I had met Ivan because he knew my story of Ivan's trip to Vietnam and the story of how that had come about. Gareth included a little detail about this story with him when he completed the form. As a result, when Ivan came to give me a shoutout, he remembered who I was, and remembered sharing his Vietnam story with me.

Stories connect people within a network and help us to remember each other. We are more likely to remember someone if we have shared a story with them and if we meet again, we will remember the story we shared.

A Story about a Story – Part 3

I naturally wanted to thank Ivan for his shoutout so I sent him a thank-you email. In the email, I mentioned that I was still grateful for the story he shared with me when we had met in 2016 and had used it when training other members of BNI. I also sent him a gift as a thank you, a copy of my first book, 'What's Your URP?'.

Christmas came and went, then I received an excited WhatsApp message from Gareth. 'Have you checked your email?'. Ivan had emailed me. He had very kindly read my book, and even more amazingly, he was very complimentary. He even asked me to send him some materials so he could promote my book to his social media followers and he did this on LinkedIn soon after. As a result of all this story development, I am very proud to have a quote from Dr Ivan Misner on the front cover of my first book.

This is the power of your narrative in your network. All of the above is linked by one great story from Ivan. The story has a life of its own. I have nurtured the story in my network, and by including it here, the story is now part of yours.

You never know where your stories are going to go, nor how long it will take for them to develop. If your story is of making a difference for others, and you share others' similar stories, over time social capital is enhanced for all involved.

Getting Things Done

We have explored the noticeable differences we want and the interactions that are involved. To realise these differences, we need to do something or make a change. The method in this book helps you take small steps and notice signs of progress. Now is the time to get things done.

At the final stage of our process, we imagine that we are a step closer to what we want. What will we notice? This usually enables a simple action plan to take shape. How does this process apply to more complex decisions? Or where we need to deliver significant change?

Houston, we have a Project.

Commander James Arthur Lovell Jr is a distinguished astronaut. In a long career, he was famous as the commander of the Apollo 13 lunar mission. When the oxygen tanks onboard their spacecraft failed, he famously reported, 'Houston, we had a problem', possibly the most famous understatement of modern times.

As portrayed in the movie *Apollo 13*, the ground crew and space crew immediately started developing a new support system to get them back to Earth. An immediate project was born. There was no time to write a plan, create a Gantt chart, or detailed specifications. The team worked out they needed to return the astronauts safely, and the mission was changed immediately so that this became the common aim of everyone involved. The team improvised a solution through a series of iterative steps and while the world held it's collective breath for three days, the astronauts returned to Earth safely.

Projects deliver outcomes following more complex activity often with multiple resources. Projects usually have a goal and a plan that will deliver the goal in a set time. The goal is defined as a major action such as to build a new runway or to plan a family holiday. This is broken down into an action plan and a timetable, and the completion of the individual tasks will result in the delivery of the project. If we stick to the timetable for each task, we will deliver on time, and we can set a budget and work within that too.

To help illustrate this, here is the typical approach to project planning and delivery.

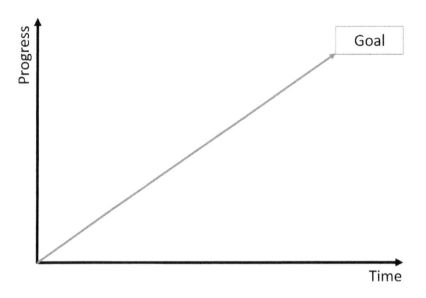

Figure 1 – The Initial Plan

We start with a goal in mind and then work out a plan to deliver this goal. In my example, this is represented by the straight line on the chart above. I have heard of many techniques to develop this plan. One of the most common is called backward planning, backward goal-setting or backward design. This is incredibly popular, and on paper very attractive. The idea is that you start with the end goal in mind, and then work backwards from there to your current point. This gives you all the steps you need to complete your plan which then sounds simple.

Unfortunately, this doesn't take account of the fact that change is happening all the time. So, while the project plan starts as linear, things will change during delivery. In real life, all project managers take account of this and will propose changes to the plan. The traditional form of delivery is illustrated in the following image:

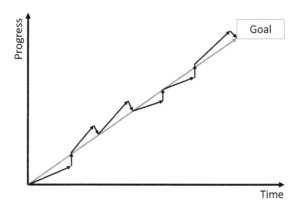

Figure 2 – Delivery Reference the Original Plan

The delivery of the original plan requires constant reference to the original plan. At each review stage, allowing for changes, the intention is to get 'back on track', get back to the plan. The original plan doesn't change unless the goal changes.

I know that many project management systems no longer try to follow this approach, however, if we look at some of the major projects in the UK we can see that this is still very common. If you consider major investments such as High Speed 2 or the third runway at Heathrow, the goal of building these is somehow fixed. The original plans having been made, the stated aim of those who want to build them is to keep returning the project to the original plan. As budgets balloon or legal obstacles are placed in their way, so the delivery teams become ever more determined to stick to the plan. Perhaps the massive increase in working from home caused by the Covid-19 pandemic will finally force a rethink?

Applying the methods I have shared here means we don't try to identify every task before we begin. We take steps and then take account of the change that is happening as we do these. We work with this when considering the differences sought to make sure we are noticing what we want.

We start with translating the goal into our list of SOMIT differences as covered in earlier chapters. Identifying these enables the first steps to be identified. These small steps will deliver progress and then we can review. We will notice the signs and signals that will inform us that we are making progress.

I am grateful to my friend John Wheeler for this model. The process is illustrated in his diagram here:

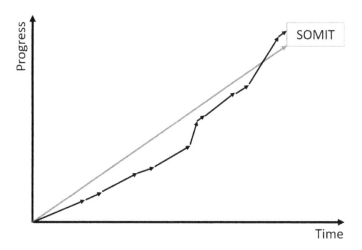

Figure 3 – Project Delivery using Solution Focused Practice

The project delivery is co-created through constant review of the differences required. At every review, reference is made to the progress made already. It was in this way that the Apollo 13 team were able to keep the astronauts alive and return them safely to Earth.

An approach to managing projects which uses this is Agile, a technique used widely in the development of software. Agile is an iterative approach to managing software development projects. Small teams make small step improvements in the software. These are released as updates or new versions. Feedback from clients is then fed into the next stage of development. These small steps are called iterations. Through the completion and release of these iterations, continuous progress is made.

The 12-month Business Plan

Every business owner is told they need a business plan. Thus, having a completed plan becomes the goal. We are told this is very important, so in our minds, we must make a Business Plan that will impress. We can look for templates online, or we might be given a template from our bank. We can include all the elements that have been added over the years. We can work with complex documents and add complexity of our own. We can easily fill 50 pages if we want to. And we will then have a 'proper' Business Plan. Is that what we really want?

The Goal – What do we want?

If we had a brilliant 12-month business plan and implemented it beautifully, what would we notice 12 months and 1 day from now? In other words, what difference do we want?

Instead of looking to write a plan, let's work on the next 12 months being the 'Best Year Ever'.

We start by visiting the future, and imagining we have what we want. In conversation, we can ask:

'Let's imagine we have delivered our Best Year Ever. We walk into the office the day after. What do you notice that tells us we have just had the Best Year Ever?'

We can expand the list of noticeable differences by asking 'what else?' until we have a long list of things we would notice. We can also explore what other stakeholders would notice. Colleagues, clients, suppliers, relatives, or specific stakeholders such as the board of directors, or the marketing team. What about friends and family? Who else is involved? We can imagine what one person would notice as they walked into the office. What would 'the Chief Executive' notice, or what would 'our biggest client' notice. In this way, we are exploring useful interactions and exploring from different perspectives.

Having explored our desired future in detail across many interactions and perspectives, a long list of noticeable differences will emerge. I often run this conversation in workshops with teams. We usually end up with many pages of flipchart paper filled with noticeable differences.

Coming back to where we are now

The next stage is to come back to where we are now, and to review the list. We ask:

'Do we notice these happening now or have they happened recently, even just a little?'

Working through the list, we always find we notice some of the differences already. This builds confidence in the team. We are already enjoying much of what would make this our Best Year Ever.

Have you ever asked people to make a change and met with resistance? When we ask a team to do something new or different, we can cause anxiety. People look at the change as being something huge. The perceived scale of the changes to make can worry them. This creates resistance which makes change harder to do or to make.

When we present others with a need for change, this process helps.

By taking the time to see if any of our desired future is happening now, we reduce the size of the change we want. It helps to build confidence if we notice the signs that we are already making progress to where we want to be. We are starting from a point that is closer already to where we want to be in 12 months.

What would we notice if we were one step closer?

Having built confidence by noticing the progress we have already made, we then look again at our lists. We identify the differences we would notice if we were one step closer to where we want to be.

We look back at the list of noticeable differences after we have had our

Best Year Ever. It is easy to select the items we will notice next. We can then identify the actions needed that will deliver these.

Following this process, we have an action plan that is short term and easy to implement. The team are aligned around the shared vision. We can confidently start on delivery immediately and we know what to look for to tell us it is working.

Take Small Steps and Review

The process of delivery involves taking small steps and having regular reviews.

We review by checking that we still want the noticeable differences identified in our first workshop. This ensures that we are taking account of the change that is happening all the time, and that has happened since we started.

We look again to see which of the differences we are noticing as we make progress. Noticing these builds confidence. Not noticing these means we need to change our activity. This process determines the next small steps.

We look at the differences we would notice if we were one more step closer to where we want to be. A new action plan emerges. The team can make progress on the delivery in an iterative way.

Example – The 5-Year Business Plan

I was approached recently to help a very successful charity. I met the Chief Executive Officer for a coffee. She told me that the Board had recently completed a strategy away day and they now wished to convert the strategy into a 5-year Business Plan. Could I help?

This is the kind of brief for which most consultants would be very grateful. The desire to add complexity means many have a process to create business plans. Creation of a 5-year business plan will involve many days of their time, they can charge a good daily rate, and the output is clear for the client. The large document produced at the end provides strong evidence of all their hard work and gives the client what they said they wanted.

With my simpler approach, I know that a 5-year Business Plan is out of date as soon as it is written, so why spend time and money creating it? The question in my mind is to find out what difference the

Business Plan will make. What does my client want?

As always, I accepted the client's goal (creation of a 5-year business plan). I started the conversation about what difference this would make.

'Let's imagine you created a fantastic five-year business plan and implemented it brilliantly. You walk into your office the day after. What do you notice that tells you you have just implemented a brilliant five-year plan?'

In accepting the client's brief, I was not jumping straight to 'action' and accepting the need they had presented, nor was I entering an argument. I was simply sense-checking to see where the need came from, and the differences this five-year business plan would make to the charity.

We explored the future state together, with me asking what others would notice. We explored the Board members' reasons for this work to be done. Having done this and taken copious notes, I then asked:

'Looking at these differences you have identified, do you notice any of them

happening now?'

My client was able to identify the differences she noticed now. This gave her confidence that there was a lot going well in her organisation.

Finally, I asked:

'So, if you were one step closer to implementing a fantastic five-year business plan, what would you notice?'

With that, she was able to identify her next steps and this, in turn, became an Action Plan.

The whole conversation took around 45 minutes. This was our first meeting.

There were strong reasons for the creation of a five-year business plan to meet the needs expressed by the Board. In 45 minutes, my client had experienced the process for herself. She commissioned me to run this project involving her team and partners and we ran workshops that followed this process. We created a 5-year Business Plan that started with a rich description of the desired future five years from now. It had a detailed Action Plan for year 1, less detail in years 2 and 3, and very little detail in years 4 and 5.

The plan was signed off by the board in record time. All staff were involved in the creation, and all were able to make immediate progress while the document was being written.

Conclusions

My intention in writing this book is to help you make life as simple as possible, but not simpler. The methods I have explained here are not easy to apply. Try them and try them again; they work.

We have created a world where to be doing something and be seen to be doing something is considered to be a good thing. I hope I have demonstrated that there is a better, simpler and more effective way.

If we start by thinking about what we want, and how to describe it, we make things easier for ourselves. We stop worrying about what we don't want. We take back control of our destinies.

We can stimulate conversations that are about what is working in our world. We can look for the resources we have within our networks that will help us. We can notice the good in people, in our immediate environment, and in the people we interact with. We can look for the stories about people making a difference and we can celebrate this. We can place problems and issues in the context they belong to. Most of the time, most of us have what we want. We are blessed with health, adequate wealth, accommodation, nourishment, education and entertainment. If we look for what contributes to these already, it is easy to find a little more of what we want.

We do not need to take action as our first step and we should not be taken in by the bold promises of large-scale change. We should not look for the most complex, risky and expensive option when there are usually easy alternatives, and if we simplify our approach, we will benefit. The beauty of making small changes is that the benefits can be vast and realised rapidly.

When we look for the differences we want and describe them in noticeable terms, we can make rapid progress in small steps. In review, we know that we are heading in the right direction.

When we look at the useful interactions that contribute to the difference we want, we find resources and support that will help us.

When we look outside of ourselves, we notice the good things that are happening all the time.

When we realise that these differences, interactions and good things are contributing to our social capital, we take control of our destinies. Our health improves, especially our mental health. We realise the value of our network to us and the importance of contributing to it. We nurture our network, we share stories, we offer praise and compliments when we notice others making a difference. This makes them feel good and makes us feel good too.

We benefit in many other ways. When we put making a difference for others before making money for ourselves, we spend less money. We no longer need to spend money on luxuries that we think make a difference for ourselves. We think about the difference the item will make before we buy it. We think about the interactions with others that we want. If we are already noticing these, we can choose to spend more wisely.

The call to action is strong within us all. Indiana Jones is still seen as the hero, and the films are still fantastic entertainment. For one final example, let me refer you to Season 7, Episode 4 of *The Big Bang Theory*. In this episode, the characters explore their favourite film, *Raiders of the Lost Ark*. It turns out that the Nazis hunting for the Ark of the Covenant would have found it without Indiana's contribution. If anything, his actions help them to find it more quickly. The outcome would have been the same whether Indiana Jones had been involved, or not.

The heroes are not the swashbucklers. The heroes are those who make a difference.

This book combines knowledge and experience from my many years of practice. It is only in the last couple of years that I have realised the power of this approach. It has taken me this long to draw the various elements together so that they work with each other as a method. I hope this book helps you find what you want, in ways that make a difference, and helps you to enjoy a life that is as simple as possible, not simpler.

Resources

If you are interested in exploring the strands woven together in this book, here are some resources which I hope you find useful.

Solution Focused Practice is closely related to Solution Focused Brief Therapy. If you search for either of these terms, you will find a local practitioner or online resources. There are many associations and organisations dedicated to the development and practice of SFP. I include a short list here:

- Solution Focused in Organisations (SFiO.org)
- United Kingdom Asssociation for Solution Focused Practice (UKASFP.org)
- SOLworld (SOLworld.net)

Wherever you are, find your local association or contact me on andrew@andrew-gibson.com to find out more about how SFP can help.

Dr Luc Isebaert worked at the Korzybski Institute (Korzybski.be).

Gregory Bateson was influential in various fields and published many books and papers. It is impossible to summarise his contributions and achievements here and there are many resources available online and in print.

Greg Vinnicombe was my friend and business associate until his untimely death in October 2015. His business partner, John Wheeler, and their team continue to train Solution Focused Practice and can be found at solutionfocused.training. For other sources of training in your area, please see the associations listed above.

Specialist Autism Services is a charity based in Bradford and Leeds, UK. Their website is specialistautismservices.org

Nick Forgham is multi-talented, and trains Shotokan Karate. His book, 'Black Belt Thinking' is available on amazon.

The 'Spotlight Effect' was first defined in the paper, 'The Spotlight Effect and the Illusion of Transparency: Egocentric Assessments of How We Are Seen by Others', first published December 1, 1999 in the journal 'Current Directions in Psychological Science' by Thomas Gilovich and Kenneth Savitsky.

Fit20 is a global fitness system based on High Intensity Resistance Training. Fit20.com

BNI is the world's largest referral based networking organisation. BNI. com. **Dr Ivan Misner**, Founder and Chief Visonary Officer of BNI, has published many books, and shares his resources via conference speeches, blogs and podcasts. His personal website is ivanmisner.com.

Paul Furlong's podcast is 'Rule the World: The Art and Power of Storytelling' and can be found on Apple Podcasts and other podcast providers

Agile Software development is widely used to deliver software projects. See agilemanifesto.org. Roy Marriott combines Solution Focused Practice with Agile and can be found at roymarriott.com.

My first book, **'What's Your URP?'** is available on amazon and is also published by Woven Word.

Ingram Content Group UK Ltd.
Milton Keynes UK
UKHW021408260323
419169UK00016B/1564